DIALING GOD

DAILY CONNECTION BOOK

Technology for the Soul™

Edite

K   A L A H

Published by
Kabbalah Centre International Inc.

155 E. 48th St., New York, NY 10017
1062 S. Robertson Blvd., Los Angeles, CA 90035

First Edition 2003

Revised Edition 2011
Second Printing 2012

ISBN: 978-157189-775-6

Printed in USA

I would like to dedicate this to my Son
Toussaint Maceo Chen
you are a Blessing in my life.

Some days when I feel like I do not want to go on,
I look at you and find that I can.
For all the times that I have been telling you that you cry too much
and that you should be strong because you are a man,
now I want to thank you for showing me
it takes great strength to be weak.

I hope you will get all the Light you need to change yourself
and the world through this book.
I will keep growing and learning how to Love you Unconditionally.
I will always be with you, no matter what.

Thank you for showing me strength through your tears.

Introduction by Kabbalist Rav Berg / 5

Hebrew-Aramaic letters & pronunciation guide / 7

Meditation for Dialing God / 11

Morning Blessings:

       Memory Meditation / 13

       Modeh Ani / 13

       Al Netilat Yadayim - Washing of the Hands / 14

       Asher Yatzar / 14

       Elohai Neshamah / 16

       The Eighteen Blessings / 18

The Letter of the Ramban / 32

Petichat Eliyahu - The Opening of Elijah the Prophet / 39

Mikveh Meditation / 51

The Ana Beko'ach / 54

       Letters of the Month / 58

       Tikkun Hanefesh / 59

       Angels of the Day / 61

The Shema Reading in the Morning / 66

Meditation for Sustenance / 77

Medition for giving Tzedakah (Charity) / 80

Meditaion for giving Ma'aser (Tithing) / 81

Meditation for Healing / 84

Blessings for Candle Lighting / 85

The Shema Reading at Bedtime / 88

Blessings Before Food / 105

Last Blessings:

        Birkat Hamazon / 108

        Me'en Shalosh / 130

        Bore Nefashot / 134

Meditation for Traveling / 135

The 72 Names of God / 136

Contact Information / 137

Glossary / 138

Of all human activity, there is nothing as innate to humanity as prayer. It is one of the few activities of the human race that has no counterpart in the animal world. Only the human race is destined to rule over the entire universe and all that is contained within it.

The kabbalistic concept of prayer is that praying gives us the opportunity to participate in the quantum dynamics of the cosmos. Because the kabbalistic system puts mankind in the center of the universe, our actions and inactions affect everything. Thus, our participation through prayer in the interconnected workings of the cosmos is the only way to ensure that our fragmented universe will once again be restored to its original unity.

Prayer is anything but a robotic tool for alleviating the hearts of the saddened and the conscience of the evildoer. Our very lives and environment depend on this very powerful instrument because it allows us to achieve control over our destinies. The hostile environment, the threatening cosmos, the natural enemies of our physical body, the degenerative process of aging — all represent the trials and tribulations that each of us faces everyday.

Life, as we experience it, is a picture of chaos and suffering from the first day that we breathe air into our physical bodies. For many of us, the struggle may begin in our mother's womb. But no matter when life starts, the bottom line reads like a broken record: chaos, misfortune, and more of the same tomorrow. Somehow, despite our reverence and belief in prayer, nothing ever really changes.

It therefore should come as no surprise that most of earth's inhabitants no longer include prayer as part of their daily routine. The time-honored ritual of prayer has not retained its magic spell in most religions. And yet, prayer with *kavanah* (the word *kavanah* stems from the word *kivune*, "direction," indicating that the mind must take a direction when reciting prayers), as practiced by our Centres all over the globe, has drawn tens of thousands to its practice — despite the inability of many to understand the meanings of the words used or, for that matter, to be capable of even reading the words. For the majority of believers, scanning has more than sufficed for them to experience the effect of prayer.

The Zohar explains that the recitation of the words themselves is not to be considered as fulfilling or accomplishing the objective of prayer, as is clearly stated in the following excerpt from *Zohar Bemidbar*: "Prayer is made up of both action and speech, and when the action is faulty, speech does not find a spot to rest in; such prayer is not prayer, and the man offering it is defective in the Upper and the Lower Worlds."

Kavanah is the directed meditation, or concentration, that accompanies the words of a prayer. It has been said that "prayer should be offered with proper *kavanah* on the words uttered in the Lord's presence."

According to the *Zohar*, *kavanah* is a significant and integral element for spiritual growth. Rav Bachye Iben Paquda remarks that prayer without concentration, or *kavanot* [*kavanot* is the plural of *kavanah*; the words can be used interchangeably], is like a body without a soul or a husk without a kernel. In essence, the kabbalist considers the words of the prayer as the body or channel for the more important aspect of *kavanot*, which can be likened to the soul of prayer.

Prayers are like us: Without a soul, both we and they are empty. Prayers said by rote, without *kavanah*, are useless. Indeed, it was Rabbi Eliezer who said, "He that makes his prayer a fixed task, his prayer is not a prayer."

The word most commonly used for "prayer" is *tefillah*, the root of which means "trivial" or "secondary." Nevertheless, although the words of prayer are secondary, they are not redundant. Just as the soul needs the body to express itself in physical existence, so does the consciousness need the words and letters of prayers. The intent in both prayer and meditation is to instill the ever-present Light in our awareness. Our prayers connect with aspects of the Light of the Creator. It is beyond our perception to understand how this works, but we can see the positive effects in our lives.

Kabbalah teaches that there are two universes, or realities: the Tree of Knowledge of Good and Evil reality and the Tree of Life reality. We live in the Tree of Knowledge reality, which is characterized by chaos, pain, and suffering. Our goal is to achieve the Tree of Life reality, which is the reality that lies beyond our limited five senses and is the reality suffused by the Lightforce.

This reality is a realm of infinite fulfillment and order. It is the source of our intuition and sixth sense, the place from which healing, pleasure, and happiness originate. We may not be able to physically touch and see this reality, but it is as undeniable as gravity and as real as the atoms in the air.

When the Lightforce reigns supreme, there is no room for chaos and disorder. The seeds and roots of all the flaws we find in our journey through life originate within the Tree of Knowledge reality, where good and evil exist side by side. When communion with the Lightforce is established, the degree of chaos and disorder in our lives will be decreased in direct proportion to the degree of our connection.

The ultimate goal of *kavanah*-meditation is a total *devekut*, a "clinging," to the Lightforce. In the Tree of Life reality, quantum control pervades the entire universe. (Quantum refers to the interconnectedness of everything.) In the Tree of Knowledge reality, our limited rational minds perceive people and things as separate entities, each possessing its own local independent reality. Our goal is to achieve a total communion with the Lightforce, thus taking a quantum leap into the Tree of Life reality, where everything is connected.

The Kabbalah Centres have already left their mark on the consciousness of millions of people. The techniques in use at the Centres as described here will certainly meet with resistance, as do all ideas that appear to conflict with existing norms. Indeed, this same reluctance to change, even to listen, is attested to every day by mankind's dismal record of dominion over the environment and daily living.

May this book be a vehicle for you to achieve an elevated state of consciousness so that you can truly become the master of your own destiny.

THE HEBREW-ARAMAIC LETTERS

The purpose of this book is to help you to make a connection to the ever-present Lightforce of the Creator. The Hebrew-Aramaic letters are a powerful tool given to us by the Creator to assist in making that connection. Since, before the time of Creation, these letters were designed to be channels for the energy of the Lightforce.

The Hebrew-Aramaic letters are channels of energy. The 72 Names of God are channels of energy built on sequences of Hebrew-Aramaic letters (see page 136 for a complete chart of the 72 Names of God).

It is not necessary to master or to even memorize the techniques contained in this book to bring profound changes to your life and to the world around you. All that is required is an open mind and an open heart.

As you let your eyes — the windows to your soul — scan the shapes and sequences of each letter in these prayers and blessings, you can be certain that your effort will ignite the power of these letters, allowing them to draw the Lightforce of the Creator into your consciousness.

There is no uniformly applied system for Hebrew-Aramaic transliteration. So in this book we have adhered to what is called: "Sephardic pronunciation" as it follows the kabbalistic method of pronunciation and also it is the easiest of use (and not to be scientifically accurate).

The Hebrew-Aramaic letters are consonants. The vowels are symbolized by the markings under or over or next to the letters. The vowels in this transliteration are as spoken in the simplest way.

The consonants below are just to give the vowels a consonant to which to relate:

a – (or ah in the end of some words) – sounds as in "jump" (represents *kamatz* and *patach*).

ai – sounds as in "chai" (only in the end of a word with the letter *Yud*).

e – (or eh in the end of some words) - sounds as in "rest" (represents *segol* and *tzere* and *sheva na*).

ee – sounds as "free" (only in some words like "*Beresheet*").

ei – sounds as "day" (only in the end of a word with the letter *Yud*).

i – sounds as in "ink" (represents *chirik*).

o – (or oh in the end of some words) - sounds as in "off" (represents *cholam* and *kamatz gadol*)

oi – sounds as in "decoy" (only in the end of a word with the letter *Yud*).

u – sounds as in "room" (represents *shuruk* and *kubutz*)

We use a comma to separate syllables (For example: "*veyit'hadar*") and to separate the sounds of two vowels (For example: "*ha'ola*"). This clarifies pronunciation, and simplifies the words.

Consonants which have a different form as the final letter in a word but sound the same:

The Letter	Letter's Name	Sounds like:	comments
ך (כ)	Kaf	k	K as in "Kenya"
ך (כ)	without dagesh	ch	As in "loch" (Scottish) - a very soft "ch" sound made from the throat.
ם (מ)	Mem	m	M as in "Mars"
ן (נ)	Nun	n	N as in "Norway"
ף (פ)	Pei	p	P as in "Panama"
ף (פ)	without dagesh	f	F as in "France"
ץ (צ)	Tzadik	tz	Tz as in "its"

The Letter	Letter's Name	Sounds like:	comments
א	Alef	a, e, i, o, u	Depend of the vowel – could be sound as "apple." Could be as vowel stop letter.
ב	Bet	b	B as in "Brazil"
ב	without dagesh	v	V as in "Venus"
ג	Gimel	g	G as in "goal" or "grand"
ד	Dalet	d	D as in "David"
ה	Hei	h	H as in "Hawaii" or could be silent when come in the end of the word
ו	Vav	v, u, o	V as in "Venus" or U as in "Saudi" or could be vowel as O (without any sound).
ז	Zayin	z	Z as in "zebra"
ח	Chet	ch	As in "loch" (Scottish) - a very soft "ch" sound made from the throat.
ט	Tet	t	T as in "Turkey"
י	Yud	i, y	I (in the end of a word) as in "Australia" Y (in the middle of a word) as in "Yugoslavia."
כ	Kaf	k	K as in "Kenya"
כ	without dagesh	ch	As in "loch" (Scottish) - a very soft "ch" sound made from the throat.

The Letter	Letter's Name	Sounds like:	comments
לֹ	Lamed	l	L as in "Libya"
מ	Mem	m	M as in "Mars"
נ	Nun	n	N as in "Norway"
ס	Samech	s	S as in "Scotland"
עַ	Ayin	a, e, i, o, u	deep throat sound (Oriental) -intermediate in standard Hebrew.
פ	Pei	p	P as in "Panama"
פ	without dagesh	f	F as in "France"
צ	Tzadik	tz	Tz as in "its"
קֻ	Kuf	k	K as in "Kenya"
ר	Resh	r	R as in "Russia"
שׁ	Shin	sh	Dot over the right side – sh as in "show."
שׂ		s	Dot over the left side - s as in "Scotland."
ת	Tav	T	T as in "Turkey."

How to Dial God — *Lamed Vav Vav*

INSIGHT

The Light is always there, never changing, forever willing and able to fulfill our every desire, to answer our every prayer. Just like the electricity in our home, it is ever-present, but we must plug into it to physically receive its many benefits.

The Name *Lamed Vav Vav* clears all obstructions preventing our prayers from reaching God. It repairs broken lines, removes interference, and establishes a secure line of communication to the Upper Worlds. But it does this only if we acknowledge that *we alone* are responsible for getting our prayers answered.

It is written that when the terrified and desperate Israelites called out to God on the banks of the Red Sea, God asked, "Why are you calling out to Me?" God's words here were merely code: He was actually telling the people that *they themselves held the power* to escape from their peril. They did not require His assistance.

In fact, God *never* answers prayers. It is we ourselves who answer our own prayers by knowing how to connect to and utilize the Divine Energy of the Creator and the God-like force in our own soul.

There are many negative forces that attempt to block and impede our prayers. We create these negative forces through our own negative behavior and unkind words. In the same way as freezing rain and ice break down power lines, our cold and bitter behavior breaks down the lines of communication to the Source of all blessings.

PURPOSE:

ARE YOU CONSTANTLY GETTING A BUSY SIGNAL WHEN YOU PRAY?

IS THERE TOO MUCH STATIC ON THS LINE?

ARE YOU CONSTANTLY GETTING CUT OFF EACH TIME YOU DIAL?

IS IT HARD TO GET AN OUTSIDE LINE?

MEDITATION

You dial. You connect. Your prayers are answered at the speed of Light.

MEDITATION FOR SPIRITUAL MEMORY

The time for this meditation is every morning at dawn

The great kabbalist Rav Chaim Vital teaches us that using the special names below in time of dawn can help us improve our spiritual memory. The amount of information exist in the universe is endless. There is no chance that we can remember everything. Using the following meditation will help us to be connected and synchronized with the Light system that will make sure we are in the right time and in the right places.

MORNING BLESSINGS

MODEH ANI

Every night, when our souls ascend to the Upper Worlds, a powerful force attempts to stop us from awakening and seeing the light of a new day. This force resides within each one of us. It is our negative side, or, what the kabbalists call our "Evil Inclination," fueled by our negative behavior from the previous day. However, the Creator gives us another chance each day to change and reveal the Light that we failed to reveal the day before. The connection of *Modeh Ani* allows us to take advantage of this opportunity. This sequence of Aramaic letters arouses our appreciation for the return of our soul to our body. This act of appreciation helps to strengthen and protect all the blessings we receive.

When you wake up, even though your hands are not clean, you can still say
the verse "modeh ani" since it does not contain one of the Holy Names.

ס"ג מ"ה ב"ן lefanecha לְפָנֶיךָ אני ani אֲנִי‏ (moda מוֹדָה :Women say) modeh מוֹדָה

bi בִּי shehechezarta שֶׁהֶחֱזַרְתָּ vekayam וְקַיָּם chai וְחַי melech מֶלֶךְ

‡emunatecha אֱמוּנָתֶךָ raba רַבָּה ◆bechemla בְּחֶמְלָה nishmati נִשְׁמָתִי

I give thanks before You, living and existing King,
for restoring my soul to me, compassionately. Great is Your trustworthiness.

WASHING OF THE HANDS

When we sleep at night, many negative forces latch onto our body. When our soul returns and reconnects with our body, it removes most of that negativity, but not from our hands. By washing our hands each morning upon waking, we accomplish three important objectives:

1) To cleanse and wash away all negative forces that cling to our hands during the night;

2) To connect ourselves to the cause and seed level of reality (proactive) and not just the effect (reactive);

3) To detach ourselves from the energy of *ani* (poor) and connect ourselves to the energy of *ashir* (rich). The last three words of this blessing are *Al Netilat Yadayim*. The first letter from each of these three words spells *ani* עֲנִי, Aramaic for "a poor person". The last 2 letters of each of these 3 words, *Ayin Lamed* עַל, *Lamed Tav* לַת, and *Yud Mem* יִם, have the same numerical value as the word *ashir* עָשִׁיר, meaning "a rich person."

> Wash your hands, go to the bathroom as necessary, and then wash your hands again. The way to wash our hands: Hold the washing vessel in your right hand and fill it with water, and then hand it over to your left hand. Then, pour the water from the left over the right and then pour water from the right onto the left. That process should be repeated a second and a third time. You should not wash them three times in a row, but alternate between right and left. Rub your hands together 3 times and raise them to the level of the eyes and say the blessing before drying the hands.

בְּרוּךְ baruch (אל)   אַתָּה Ata (רוזם)   יְהֹוָאדֹנֵיאהֹדונֵהי Adonai (וזגן)

אֱלֹהֵינוּ Elohenu (ילה) (ארך)   מֶלֶךְ melech (אפים)   הָעוֹלָם ha'olam (ורב) (וזסד)

אֲשֶׁר asher (ואמת)   קִדְּשָׁנוּ kideshanu (נצר וזסד)   בְּמִצְוֹתָיו bemitzvotav (לאלפים)

וְצִוָּנוּ vetzivanu (נשא עון)   עַל al (ופשע)   נְטִילַת netilat (וזטאה)   יָדָיִם yadayim (ונקה:)

Blessed are You, Lord, our God, the King of the world,
Who has sanctified us with His commandments and obliges us with the washing of the hands.

ASHER YATZAR

There are 45 words in *Asher Yatzar*, numerical value of Adam. Reciting *Asher Yatzar* after each time we have been to the bathroom connects us to the original spiritual DNA and blueprint of a human being.

We may wake up in the morning feeling depleted of spiritual energy, depressed, fearful, moody, or even full of dread for the day to come. Through the power of *Asher Yatzar*, we inject the Light of Creation into our immune system; strengthening and boosting it so that we become filled with Light and spiritually recharged for the entire day.

יכה Elohenu אֱלֹהֵינוּ   Adonai יְהֹוָה‎אדנ‎יאהדונהי   Ata אַתָּה   baruch בָּרוּךְ

et אֶת   yatzar יָצַר   asher אֲשֶׁר   ha'olam הָעוֹלָם   melech מֶלֶךְ

(מצוות)◆   תרי"ג   במילוי   bechochma בְּחָכְמָה   מ"ה   ha'adam הָאָדָם

vo בּוֹ   קנ"א ב"ן, יהוה אלהים יהוה אדני, מילוי קס"א וס"ג, מ"ה ברבוע וע"ב ע"ה   uvara וּבָרָא

chalulim חֲלוּלִים   וְחֲלוּלִים chalulim   nekavim נְקָבִים◆   nekavim נְקָבִים

galuy גָּלוּי   וז"פ אל, רי"ו ול"ב נתיבות החכמה, רמ"ח (אברים), עסמ"ב וט"ז אותיות פשוטות.◆

לכב ,ב"ן   chevodecha כְּבוֹדֶךָ   chise כִּסֵּא   lifnei לִפְנֵי   veyadu'a וְיָדוּעַ

yisatem יִסָּתֵם   יוהך, מ"א אותיות דפשוט, דמילוי ודמילוי דמילוי דאהיה ע"ה   she'im שֶׁאִם

דפשוט אותיות מ"א ,יוהך im אִם   oh אוֹ   mehem מֵהֶם   דאגה ,אהבה echad אֶחָד

דאגה ,אהבה echad אֶחָד   yipate'ach יִפָּתֵחַ   ע"ה דאהיה דמילוי ודמילוי דמילוי

afilu אֲפִלּוּ   lehitkayem לְהִתְקַיֵּם   efshar אֶפְשָׁר   ei אִי   mehem מֵהֶם

Adonai יְהֹוָה‎אדנ‎יאהדונהי   Ata אַתָּה   baruch בָּרוּךְ◆   echat אַחַת   sha'a שָׁעָה

la'asot לַעֲשׂוֹת: umafli וּמַפְלִיא   basar בָּשָׂר   chol כָּל יכי   rofe רוֹפֵא

Blessed are You, Lord, our God, the King of the world, Who made man with wisdom and created in him many openings and many cavities. It is obvious and known before Your Throne of Glory that should any one of them become blocked or should any one of them break open, then it would be impossible to remain alive for even one hour. Blessed are You, Lord, the Healer of all flesh and Who amazes by what He does.

ELOHAI NESHAMAH: CONNECTING WITH OUR SOUL

Kabbalah teaches us that there are five main levels of our soul: *Nefesh, Ruach, Neshamah, Chaya* and *Yechida*. In our day-to-day lives, most of us are not fully connected to all five levels. An umbilical-like cord constantly runs through the five levels of the soul, feeding us the minimum amount of Light we need to keep the "pilot light" glimmering in our soul. We recite *Elohai Neshamah* every morning to connect our conscious mind to the five levels of our soul so that we can awaken our true purpose and meaning in life.

The name of a person is not merely a word; it is also the spiritual connection to the soul. Each letter of a name is part of the spiritual genetic alphabet that infuses the soul with the particular form of energy that the name creates. The power of this blessing is that it tunnels through the Upper Worlds and creates a connection to all five parts of our soul. We deepen our connection to this prayer by combining our Hebrew name with the word *Neshamah* נשמה (soul). To merge your name with Neshamah, from right to left, insert the first letter of your name followed by the first letter of *Neshamah*. Then insert the second letter of your name followed by the second letter of *Neshamah*, and so on. Meditate on the entire sequence of letters before connecting to the prayer. For example, with the name Yehuda (יהודה), the combination will look as follows:

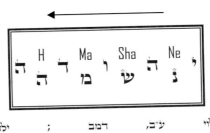

(Pause   here)   יְלה   ;   רמב   ע"ב,   מילוי   Elohai אֱלֹהַי

(five   aspects   of   the   collective   *Atzilut, Beriah, Yetzirah* and *Asiyah*)   neshamah נְשָׁמָה

♦(*Chayah* from *Atzilut*)   tehora טְהוֹרָה   (in the soul of *Adam*)   bi בִּי   shenatata שֶׁנָּתַתָּ

My God, the soul that You have given in me is pure.

◆(*Neshamah* from *Beriah*) בְּרָאתָהּ verata אַתָּה Ata

◆(*Ruach* from *Yetzirah*) יְצַרְתָּהּ yetzarta אַתָּה Ata

◆(*Nefesh* from *Asiyah*) בִּי bi נְפַחְתָּהּ nefachta אַתָּה Ata

וְאַתָּה veAta שדי בְּקִרְבִּי bekirbi מְשַׁמְּרָהּ meshamera וְאַתָּה veAta

בִּי bi וּלְהַחֲזִירָהּ ulhachazira מִמֶּנִּי mimeni לִטְּלָהּ litela עָתִיד atid

שֶׁהַנְּשָׁמָה shehaneshamah זְמַן zeman יל כָּל kol לָבוֹא lavo לֶעָתִיד le'atid

בְּקִרְבִּי vekirbi שדי מוֹדֶה modeh אֲנִי ani לְפָנֶיךָ lefanecha ס"ג מ"ה ב"ן

יְהֹוָה Adonai אֱלֹהַי Elohai מילוי ע"ב, דמב ; ילה

וֵאלֹהֵי velohei לכב ; מילוי ע"ב, דמב ; ילה אֲבוֹתַי avotai רִבּוֹן ribon יהוה עסמ"ב

כָּל kol יל הַמַּעֲשִׂים hama'asim ◆ אֲדוֹן adon אני כָּל kol יל

הַנְּשָׁמוֹת haneshamot ◆ בָּרוּךְ baruch אַתָּה Ata יְהֹוָה Adonai

הַמַּחֲזִיר hamachazir נְשָׁמוֹת neshamot לִפְגָרִים lifgarim מֵתִים metim ◆

You have formed it. You have created it. You have breathed it into me.
And You preserve it within me. You shall eventually take it away from me yet return it to me in the coming future.
As long as the soul is within me, I am grateful to You, Lord, my God and the God of my fathers, the Governor
of all actions. The Master of all souls. Blessed are You, Lord, Who restores souls to dead corpses.

THE EIGHTEEN BLESSINGS

The purpose of the Eighteen Blessings is to reconnect our soul to our physical body after it has been almost totally disconnected during the previous night's sleep. All of us are blessed with various gifts that, most of the time we do not appreciate, such as the connection of our soul to our body. Unfortunately, most of us only start to appreciate our gifts once we have lost them. Through the power of these Eighteen Blessings, we can inject a proactive energy force of appreciation, which, in turn, protects and preserves all that we hold dear.

THE FIRST BLESSING - DISTINGUISHES BETWEEN DAY AND NIGHT

The greatest gift we have as human beings is the power of free will. The phrase "distinguishing between day and night" refers to the ability we have to choose the Light of the Creator over darkness or good over evil. By saying this blessing, we are given clarity to see these two opposing forces that are usually concealed from us.

יכה Elohenu אֱלֹהֵינוּ Adonai יְהֹוָאדניהאהדונהי Ata אַתָּה baruch בָּרוּךְ

ושר אבניתך, hanoten הַנּוֹתֵן ha'olam הָעוֹלָם melech מֶלֶךְ

; ע"ה וויים, אהיה אהיה יהוה vina בִּינָה מלאך גבריאל = ע"ה שכוי lasechvi לַשֶּׂכְוִי

lehavchin לְהַבְוִזִין ארני = ללה, וס"ת (sweetening the night's judgment) ס"ג ר"ת מילוי

בִּין ben יוֹם yom ע"ה נגד, מזבוח, זן, אל יהוה uven וּבֵין layla לַיְלָה מלה ; ר"ת = ג"פ יהוה.

Blessed are You, Lord, our God,
the King of the world, Who gives the rooster the understanding to distinguish between day and night.

THE SECOND BLESSING - GIVES SIGHT TO THE BLIND

King David said: "We have eyes, but see not. We have ears, but hear not." Too often, we are blinded by a lucrative opportunity or we fail to anticipate the chaos of an impending situation. The real power of this blessing is that it helps heighten our senses of perception and intuition so that we can see the truths that are normally concealed from us.

ילה Elohenu אֱלֹהֵינוּ   Adonai יְהוָֹה־אדני־יאהדונהי   Ata אַתָּה   baruch בָּרוּךְ

ivrim עִוְרִים   poke'ach פּוֹקֵחַ   ha'olam הָעוֹלָם   melech מֶלֶךְ

Blessed are You, Lord, our God, King of the world, Who gives sight to the blind.

THE THIRD BLESSING - RELEASES THOSE WHO ARE BOUND

Often we become prisoners of our jobs, our mortgage payments, our relationships, our careers, or even other people's perceptions of us. In essence, to one degree or another, everyone is a prisoner, held captive by his Desire to Receive for the Self Alone. The energy that emanates from this blessing has the power to release us from the clutches of this powerful and self-destructive desire.

ילה Elohenu אֱלֹהֵינוּ   Adonai יְהוָֹה־אדני־יאהדונהי   Ata אַתָּה   baruch בָּרוּךְ

asurim אֲסוּרִים   matir מַתִּיר   ha'olam הָעוֹלָם   melech מֶלֶךְ

Blessed are You, Lord, our God, King of the world, Who releases those who are bound.

THE FOURTH BLESSING – STRAIGHTENS THOSE WHO ARE BENT OVER

The inner meaning of this blessing pertains to the often skewed view we have of the world and the people around us. Our self-centered ego distorts our perception of reality to the point where everyone else appears crooked, imperfect, and wrong. This particular sequence of Aramaic letters has the power to imbue us with acceptance and understanding so that we can transform the negative part of our character which perceives others as bent.

יכה   Elohenu   אֱלֹהֵינוּ   Adonai   יְהֹוָהאדניאהדונהי   Ata   אַתָּה   baruch   בָּרוּךְ

:kefufim   כְּפוּפִים   zokef   זוֹקֵף   ha'olam   הָעוֹלָם   melech   מֶלֶךְ

Blessed are You, Lord, our God, King of the world, Who straightens those who are bent over.

THE FIFTH BLESSING - CLOTHES THE NAKED

Kabbalah explains that the body is the clothing of the soul. Just as a negative person cannot change his character by donning an expensive suit, we cannot bring about personal change or lasting fulfillment without connecting to a world beyond our body consciousness. The sequence of letters in this blessing gives us the power to rise above our body consciousness and connect with our soul consciousness.

יכה   Elohenu   אֱלֹהֵינוּ   Adonai   יְהֹוָהאדניאהדונהי   Ata   אַתָּה   baruch   בָּרוּךְ

:arumim   עֲרוּמִים   malbish   מַלְבִּישׁ   ha'olam   הָעוֹלָם   melech   מֶלֶךְ

Blessed are You, Lord, our God, King of the world, Who clothes the naked.

THE SIXTH BLESSING - GIVES STRENGTH TO THE WEARY

We often try to affect positive change within ourselves. We attempt to face down our fears, rid ourselves of anger, and overcome our jealousies. But Satan, a negative intelligence, battles us from the inside, and can prevent these changes from happening. The sequence of letters in this blessing gives us that extra help and energy we need to defeat Satan.

melech מֶלֶךְ יכה Elohenu אֱלֹהֵינוּ Adonai יְהֹוָאדֹנָיאהדונהי Ata אַתָּה baruch בָּרוּךְ

נכך ko'ach כֹּחַ laya'ef לַיָּעֵף ושׂר, אבגיתץ hanoten הַנּוֹתֵן ha'olam הָעוֹלָם

Blessed are You, Lord, our God, King of the world, Who gives strength to the weary.

THE SEVENTH BLESSING - KEEPS THE LAND OVER THE WATER

The kabbalists teach that before the creation of the world, water filled all of reality and existence. Water is a physical expression of the energy force of mercy and the Lightforce of the Creator, also known as the Desire to Share. Physical matter has the inherent essence of the Desire to Receive, represented by the creation of the land on our planet. God created a delicate balance between the Desire to Share and the Desire to Receive, manifested in the balance between the water and the land. This blessing helps us achieve and maintain this balance.

יכה Elohenu אֱלֹהֵינוּ Adonai יְהֹוָאדֹנָיאהדונהי Ata אַתָּה baruch בָּרוּךְ

ע"ה אלהים דההן ha'aretz הָאָרֶץ roka רוֹקַע ha'olam הָעוֹלָם melech מֶלֶךְ

al עַל hamayim הַמָּיִם

Blessed are You, Lord, our God, King of the world, Who keeps land over the water.

THE EIGHTH BLESSING - PROVIDES FOR THE FOOTSTEPS OF MAN

When a person embarks on a spiritual path, he or she will inevitably face obstacles and challenges along the way. This particular sequence of Aramaic letters gives us the power of certainty, to know that the spiritual path we are on is the correct one, even when the road before us is temporarily dim.

יכה   Elohenu אֱלֹהֵינוּ   Adonai יְהֹוָ אֲדֹנָי אֲדֹנָי   Ata אַתָּה   baruch בָּרוּךְ

gaver גָּבֶר   mitz'adei מִצְעֲדֵי   hamechin הַמֵּכִין   ha'olam הָעוֹלָם   melech מֶלֶךְ

Blessed are You, Lord, our God, King of the world, Who provides for the footsteps of man.

THE NINTH BLESSING - PROVIDES FOR ALL MY NEEDS

We do not recite this blessing on *Tisha B'Av* (9th of Av) or on *Yom Kippur*.

This ancient sequence of letters ensures that we receive what our soul truly desires and not what our short-term reactive impulses cause us to crave.

יכה   Elohenu אֱלֹהֵינוּ   Adonai יְהֹוָ אֲדֹנָי אֲדֹנָי   Ata אַתָּה   baruch בָּרוּךְ

להמתיק דיני ע"ה דלהלן) = אלף למד אלף למד לבוד [אל א' = יהוה ד' אותיות והכולל ואל ב' = ייא"י דס"ג]   ע"ע (ע"ע) עַע   she'asa שֶׁעָשָׂה   ha'olam הָעוֹלָם   melech מֶלֶךְ

עַה = אלהים דיודין וה' אותיות   tzorki צָרְכִּי   יכי   kol כָּל   li לִי   אלהים אותיות וה'

Blessed are You, Lord, our God, King of the world, Who provides for all my needs

THE TENTH BLESSING - STRENGTHENS ISRAEL WITH MIGHT

In Aramaic, the word for "strength" is *Gevurah*. *Gevurah* has the same numerical value (216) as the three-letter sequences of the 72 Names of God (72 x 3 = 216), which helps us achieve mind over matter and overcome our reactive nature. Another secret can be found in the last three words of the blessing. The first three letters of the last three words (*Alef* א, *Yud* י, and *Bet* ב) have the same numerical value (13) as the Aramaic word for *Ahavah* (אהבה) which means "love." If we have love in our lives, we will always have the ability to tap into the power of the 72 Names of God.

יכה Elohenu אֱלֹהֵינוּ Adonai יְהֹוָ֑הֿאֲדֹנָיֿאהדונהי Ata אַתָּה baruch בָּרוּךְ

Yisrael יִשְׂרָאֵל ozer אֹוֵ֑ר ha'olam הָעֹולָם melech מֶלֶךְ

 רי״ו ; ר״ת = אהבה, אוזר, דאגה‪:‬ bigvura בִּגְבוּרָה‪:‬

Blessed are You, Lord, our God, King of the world, Who strengthens Israel with might

THE ELEVENTH BLESSING - CROWNS ISRAEL WITH SPLENDOR

The word for "splendor" in Aramaic is *Tifara*, from the root *Tiferet*. *Tiferet* is the *Sefirah* or the specific dimension that connects the Upper Worlds to our physical world. The sequence of letters that make up this blessing gives us the ability to capture and store the Light—like a portable battery that can fuel us—even after we close the *Siddur*.

יכה Elohenu אֱלֹהֵינוּ Adonai יְהֹוָ֑הֿאֲדֹנָיֿאהדונהי Ata אַתָּה baruch בָּרוּךְ

‪:‬betifara בְּתִפְאָרָה Yisrael יִשְׂרָאֵל oter עֹוטֵר ha'olam הָעֹולָם melech מֶלֶךְ

Blessed are You, Lord, our God, King of the world, Who crowns Israel with splendor.

THE TWELFTH BLESSING - DID NOT MAKE ME A GENTILE/GENTILE WOMAN

On the surface level, this blessing appears to be discriminatory. Kabbalistically, the word gentile has nothing to do with a person's religious affiliation. Rather, it is a code word which represents someone who does not have a powerful and intense Desire to Receive. This blessing ignites our desire for spiritual growth, inner change, and positive transformation.

יכה Elohenu אֱלֹהֵינוּ Adonai יְהֹוָאדְנִיאהדונהי Ata אַתָּה baruch בָּרוּךְ

:goi גּוֹי asani עָשַׂנִי shelo שֶׁלֹּא ha'olam הָעוֹלָם melech מֶלֶךְ

:Women say יכה Elohenu אֱלֹהֵינוּ Adonai יְהֹוָאדְנִיאהדונהי Ata אַתָּה baruch בָּרוּךְ

:goya גּוֹיָה asani עָשַׂנִי shelo שֶׁלֹּא ha'olam הָעוֹלָם melech מֶלֶךְ

Blessed are You, Lord, our God, King of the world, Who did not make me a gentile / gentile woman.

THE THIRTEENTH BLESSING - DID NOT MAKE ME A SLAVE/MAIDSERVANT

This blessing gives us the support we need so that we are not governed and held captive by our reactive nature and the material world.

יכה Elohenu אֱלֹהֵינוּ Adonai יְהֹוָאדְנִיאהדונהי Ata אַתָּה baruch בָּרוּךְ

:aved עֶבֶד asani עָשַׂנִי shelo שֶׁלֹּא ha'olam הָעוֹלָם melech מֶלֶךְ

:Women say יכה Elohenu אֱלֹהֵינוּ Adonai יְהֹוָאדְנִיאהדונהי Ata אַתָּה baruch בָּרוּךְ

:shifcha שִׁפְחָה asani עָשַׂנִי shelo שֶׁלֹּא ha'olam הָעוֹלָם melech מֶלֶךְ

Blessed are You, Lord, our God, King of the world, Who did not make me a slave / maidservant.

THE FOURTEENTH BLESSING – DID NOT MAKE ME A WOMAN/ MADE ME ACCORDING TO HIS WILL

Although this blessing appears to be chauvinistic, it is not. Kabbalistically, the inherent energy of the dimension of *Zeir Anpin* (comprising the *Sefirot* of *Chesed* to *Yesod*)--the pipeline through which the Light flows from the Upper Worlds into our world--is masculine. *Malchut*, our world has an inherent feminine energy. This prayer ignites appreciation for our ability to generate spiritual Light through the two energy forces of male and female, and helps the two halves of the soul--male and female--to unite.

יכה אֱלֹהֵינוּ Elohenu   Adonai יְהֹוָה (אדני יאהדונהי)   Ata אַתָּה   baruch בָּרוּךְ

isha אִשָּׁה asani עָשַׂנִי shelo שֶׁלֹּא ha'olam הָעוֹלָם melech מֶלֶךְ

kirtzono כִּרְצוֹנוֹ she'asani שֶׁעָשַׂנִי baruch בָּרוּךְ   :Women   say

Blessed are You, Lord, our God, King of the world, Who did not make me a woman. /
Blessed is He Who made me according to His Will.

THE FIFTEENTH BLESSING - REMOVES THE BOND OF SLEEP FROM MY EYES

Kabbalists have said that humanity has been asleep for 2000 years. Unfortunately, some people live their entire lives asleep. They never raise their level of consciousness, and fail to affect true inner change. The Aramaic letters in this blessing help to awaken us from that coma.

יכה Elohenu אֱלֹהֵינוּ   Adonai יְהֹוָה (אדני יאהדונהי)   Ata אַתָּה baruch בָּרוּךְ

chevlei וְחֶבְלֵי hama'avir הַמַּעֲבִיר ha'olam הָעוֹלָם melech מֶלֶךְ

me'afapai מֵעַפְעַפָּי utnuma וּתְנוּמָה מ"ה ריבוע me'enai מֵעֵינַי shena שֵׁנָה

This blessing does not end here but in the end of the next section ("*gomel chasadim tovim le'amo Yisrael*"), so that is why we don't answer AMEN here.

Blessed are You, Lord, our God,
King of the world, Who removes the bonds of sleep from my eyes and slumber from my eyelids.

VIHI RATZON

This prayer helps us to remove the forces of negativity that lie within us.

וִיהִי vihi רָצוֹן ratzon מהש ע"ה, ע"ב ברמבוע קס"א ע"ה, אל שדי ע"ה מִלְפָנֶיךָ milfanecha

יְהֹוָואדנילאהדונהי Adonai אֱלֹהַי Elohai מ"ה ב"ן ס"ג ; ילה, דמב, ע"ב מילוי

וֵאלֹהֵי velohei לכב ; מילוי ע"ב, דמב ; ילה אֲבוֹתַי avotai שֶׁתַּרְגִּילֵנִי shetargileni

בְּתוֹרָתֶךָ betoratecha◆ וְתַדְבִּיקֵנִי vetadbikeni בְּמִצְוֹתֶיךָ bemitzvoteicha◆

וְאַל ve'al תְּבִיאֵנִי tevi'eni לִידֵי lidei חֵטְא chet◆ וְלֹא velo לִידֵי lidei

עָוֹן avon◆ וְלֹא velo לִידֵי lidei נִסָּיוֹן nisayon◆ וְלֹא velo לִידֵי lidei

בִזָּיוֹן vizayon◆ וְתַרְחִיקֵנִי vetarchikeni מִיֵּצֶר miyetzer הָרָע hara◆

וְתַדְבִּיקֵנִי vetadbikeni בְּיֵצֶר beyetzer הַטּוֹב hatov וְכוֹף vechof אֶת et

יִצְרִי yitzri לְהִשְׁתַּעְבֶּד lehisht'abed לָךְ lach◆ וּתְנֵנִי utneni הַיּוֹם hayom

וּבְכָל uvchol יוֹם yom ע"ה נגד, מזבוח, זן, אל יהוה, לכב בְ"ן ; ע"ה נגד, מזבוח, זן, אל יהוה

לְחֵן lechen מזוי, מילוי, ברמבוע מ"ה ; ע"ב וּלְחֶסֶד ulchesed רמבוע יהוה מ"ה

וּלְרַחֲמִים ulrachamim בְּעֵינֶיךָ be'enecha ע"ה קס"א ; רמבוע מ"ה

וּבְעֵינֵי uv'enei רמבוע מ"ה כָּל chol ילי רוֹאָי ro'ai◆ וְגָמְלֵנִי vegomleni

וַחֲסָדִים chasadim טוֹבִים tovim◆ בָּרוּךְ baruch אַתָּה Ata יְהֹוָואדנילאהדונהי Adonai

גּוֹמֵל gomel וַחֲסָדִים chasadim טוֹבִים tovim לְעַמּוֹ le'amo יִשְׂרָאֵל Yisrael:

And may it be Your will, Lord, our God and God of our fathers, that You accustom me to Your Torah and cause me to cleave to Your precepts, and do not bring me to the hands of sin, iniquity, temptation, nor shame. And cause me to distance myself from the Evil Inclination, and cling me to the Good Inclination, and compel my will to be subservient to You. Grant me this day and every day, grace, loving kindness, and mercy in Your sight and in the sight of all that behold me, and bestow upon me loving kindness. Blessed are You, Lord, Who bestows loving kindness on His people Israel.

Yehi Ratzon

Too often we attract negative people and unfavorable situations into our lives. We find ourselves in the wrong place at the wrong time. We do business with the wrong people. Here, we gain the ability to remove all external negative events from intruding into our lives. We also remove eleven distinct areas of negativity that can invade our environment.

milfanecha **מִלְפָנֶיךָ** מהע ע"ה, ע"ב ברריבוע קס"א ע"ה, אל שדי ע"ה ratzon **רָצוֹן** yehi **יְהִי**

velohei **וֵאלֹהֵי** ; יכה ; דמב ע"ב, מילוי **אֱלֹהֵי** Elohai אהדונהי**יְהֹוָואדנה**י ב"ן מ"ה ס"ג

hayom **הַיּוֹם** shetatzileni **שֶׁתַּצִּילֵנִי** avotai **אֲבוֹתַי** ; יכה ; דמב ע"ב, מילוי ; לכב

vayom **וְיוֹם** ע"ה נגד, מוזבוה, זך, אל יהוה yom **יוֹם** לכב, ב"ן uvchol **וּבְכָל** ע"ה נגד, מוזבוה, זך, אל יהוה

me'azei **מֵעַזֵּי** אל יהוה, זך, מוזבוה, נגד ע"ה אלהים אדני אהיה, ע"ה

panim **פָּנִים** ume'azut **וּמֵעַזּוּת** fanim **פָּנִים** me'adam **מֵאָדָם** ra **רָע**◆

mishachen **מִשָּׁכֵן** ra **רָע** mechaver **מֵחָבֵר** ra **רָע**◆ miyetzer **מִיֵּצֶר** ra **רָע**◆

hara **הָרָע** מ"ה ריבוע me'ayin **מֵעַיִן** ra **רָע**◆ mipega **מִפֶּגַע**◆

kashe **קָשֶׁה**◆ midin **מִדִּין** hara **הָרָע**◆ umilashon **וּמִלָּשׁוֹן**

shehu **שֶׁהוּא** ben **בֵּן** kashe **קָשֶׁה**◆ din **דִּין** umiba'al **וּמִבַּעַל**

berit **בְּרִית**: ven **בֵּן** she'eno **שֶׁאֵינוֹ** uven **וּבֵין** berit **בְּרִית**◆ ven **בֵּן**

May it be Your will, Lord our God and God of our forefathers, to save me this day and every day from an arrogant man and from arrogance, from an evil man, from the Evil Inclination, from an evil companion, from an evil neighbor, from an evil happening, from evil eye, and from evil speech, from harsh judgment, and a harsh opponent, whether he be a son of the covenant or not a son of the covenant.

BLESSINGS OF THE TORAH

The next three blessings are known as *Birkot haTorah* (Blessings of the Torah).

THE SIXTEENTH BLESSING -TEACHINGS OF THE TORAH

The kabbalists teach that without a connection to the Torah, we do not stand a chance affecting genuine positive change in our lives or in the world around us. According to Kabbalah, reference to the Torah refers to spiritual work and spiritual study, and to using spiritual tools. This blessing connects us to the inner essence of the Torah giving us the energy and fuel we need to ignite all the other blessings we have recited, and to imbue our lives with passion and spiritual energy.

Adonai יְהֹוָ֑ה אֲדֹנָיאיאהדונהי	Ata אַתָּה	baruch בָּרוּךְ
ha'olam הָעוֹלָם	melech מֶלֶךְ יכה	Elohenu אֱלֹהֵינוּ
bemitzvotav בְּמִצְוֹתָיו	kideshanu קִדְּשָׁנוּ	asher אֲשֶׁר
torah תּוֹרָה ראה	divrei דִּבְרֵי	al עַל vetzivanu וְצִוָּנוּ

According to the Ari: We answer AMEN after this blessing, as this is a separate blessing from the next one.

Blessed are You, Lord, our God, King of the world,

Who has sanctified us with His commandments and obliged us regarding the teachings of the Torah.

The Seventeenth Blessing - Teaches Torah to the Nation

We say this blessing with the consciousness to help everyone make a connection to the energy of the Torah. This is our opportunity to genuinely care about others and to share the Light of the Creator - one of the most powerful ways to transform our reactive nature into a proactive one.

וְהַעֲרֶב veha'arev נָא na יְהֹוָה Adonai אֱלֹהֵינוּ Elohenu יכה

אֶת et דִּבְרֵי divrei ראה תוֹרָתְךָ toratcha בְּפִינוּ befinu

וּבְפִיפִיּוֹת uv'fifiyot עַמְּךָ amecha בֵּית bet ב״פ ראה יִשְׂרָאֵל Yisrael

וְנִהְיֶה venih'ye אֲנַחְנוּ anachnu וְצֶאֱצָאֵינוּ vetze'etza'enu

(You should meditate for your children to be righteous, connected to the *Torah* and to the Light)

וְצֶאֱצָאֵי vetze'etza'ei צֶאֱצָאֵינוּ tze'etza'enu וְצֶאֱצָאֵי vetze'etza'ei

עַמְּךָ amecha בֵּית bet ב״פ ראה יִשְׂרָאֵל Yisrael כֻּלָּנוּ kulanu

יוֹדְעֵי yod'ei שְׁמֶךָ shemecha וְלוֹמְדֵי velomdei תוֹרָתְךָ toratcha

לִשְׁמָהּ lishma בָּרוּךְ baruch אַתָּה Ata יְהֹוָה Adonai

הַמְלַמֵּד hamelamed תוֹרָה torah לְעַמּוֹ le'amo יִשְׂרָאֵל Yisrael

And sweeten for us, Lord, our God, the words of Your Torah in our mouths and the mouths of Your Nation, the House of Israel. And may we and our offspring, and the offspring of our offspring, and the offspring of all Your Nation, the House of Israel, all of us know Your Names and be learners of Your Torah for its own sake. Blessed are You, Lord, Who teaches the Torah to His Nation, Israel.

THE EIGHTEENTH BLESSING - GIVES THE TORAH

The Aramaic word *chai* חי ("life") has the numerical value of 18. This blessing connects us to the Tree of Life, (*Etz HaChayim* – עץ החיים) the dimension where only fulfillment, order, and endless bliss exist.

בָּרוּך baruch אַתָּה Ata יְהֹוָה Adonai אֱלֹהֵינוּ Elohenu יכה

מֶלֶךְ melech הָעוֹלָם ha'olam אֲשֶׁר asher בָּחַר bachar

בָּנוּ banu מִכָּל mikol ילי הָעַמִּים ha'amim וְנָתַן venatan

לָנוּ lanu אלהים, אהיה ארני אֶת et תּוֹרָתוֹ torato◆ בָּרוּך baruch

אַתָּה Ata יְהֹוָה Adonai נוֹתֵן noten אבגיתץ, ושר הַתּוֹרָה hatorah:

*Blessed are You, Lord, our God, King of the world, Who has chosen us from among
all the nations and has given us His Torah. Blessed are You, Lord, Who gives the Torah.*

THE BLESSING OF THE KOHANIM

Finishing the Eighteen Blessings, we make an immediate connection to the Torah. The verses that we recite are the blessings of the priests (*Kohanim*). In ancient times, when the *Kohen* blessed the congregation in the Temple, he used the formula *Yud, Yud, Yud* ייי one of the 72 Names of God. Each of the following three sentences begins with a *Yud*. When we recite this prayer, we activate and reveal tremendous powers of healing in our lives.

וַיְדַבֵּר vaydaber ראה יְהֹוָה Adonai אֶל־ el

מֹשֶׁה Moshe מהע, ע"ב בריבוע קס"א, אל שדי, ד"פ אלהים ע"ה לֵאמֹר lemor:

"And the Lord spoke to Moses and said:

banav בָּנָיו ve'el וְאֶל־ Aharon אַהֲרֹן el אֶל־ ראה daber דַּבֵּר

מ"ה ריבוע יהוה ריבוע יהוה tevarchu תְּבָרְכוּ הֵי ko כֹּה lemor לֵאמֹר

lahem לָהֶם amor אָמוֹר Yisrael יִשְׂרָאֵל benei בְּנֵי et אֶת־

(Right - *Chesed*)

veyishmerecha וְיִשְׁמְרֶךָ Adonai יְהֹוָואֲדֹנִייאהדונהי yevarechecha יְבָרֶכְךָ

ר"ת = יהוה ; וס"ת = מ"ה

(Left - *Gevurah*)

panav פָּנָיו | Adonai יְהֹוָואֲדֹנִייאהדונהי ויו ויו זין ויו כף ya'er יָאֵר

אֶלֶיךָ elecha בפסוק אותיות יהה ; מנד vichuneka וִיחֻנֶּךָּ elecha אֵלֶיךָ

(Central - *Tiferet*)

elecha אֵלֶיךָ panav פָּנָיו | Adonai יְהֹוָואֲדֹנִייאהדונהי yisa יִשָּׂא

בפסוק תיבות האא shalom שָׁלוֹם lecha לְךָ veyasem וְיָשֵׂם וְיָשֵׂם

(*Malchut*)

Yisrael יִשְׂרָאֵל benei בְּנֵי al עַל־ shemi שְׁמִי et אֶת־ vesamu וְשָׂמוּ

avarchem אֲבָרְכֵם אני va'ani וַאֲנִי

Speak to Aaron and his sons saying: So shall you bless the Children of Israel, Say to them:
May the Lord bless you and protect you.
May the Lord enlighten His countenance for you and give you grace.
May the Lord lift His countenance towards you and give you peace.
And they shall place My Name upon the Children of Israel and I shall bless them.

THE LETTER OF THE RAMBAN (RAV MOSES NACHMANIDES 1194-1270)

The following letter was written by the Ramban to his son, teaching him humility and modesty. The Ramban instructed his son to read this letter at least once a week and promised him that every day he reads this letter all his prayers will be answered. He also said that all who say it will be protected from harm or suffering and they are promised their share in the World to Come.

שְׁמַע shema בְּנִי beni מוּסַר musar אָבִיךָ avicha, וְאַל־ ve'al תִּטֹּשׁ titosh

תּוֹרַת torat אִמֶּךָ imecha. תִּתְנַהֵג titnaheg תָּמִיד tamid לְדַבֵּר ledaber

כָּל kol דְּבָרֶיךָ devarecha בְּנַחַת benachat לְכָל lechol אָדָם adam

וּבְכָל uvchol עֵת et, וּבָזֶה uvaze תִּנָּצֵל tinatzel מִן min הַכַּעַס haka'as,

שֶׁהִיא shehi מִדָּה mida רָעָה ra'a לְהַחֲטִיא lehachati בְּנֵי benei אָדָם adam.

וְכֵן vechen אָמְרוּ amru רַבּוֹתֵינוּ rabotenu ז"ל zal: כָּל kol הַכּוֹעֵס hako'es כָּל kol

מִינֵי minei גֵּיהִנָּם Gehinom שׁוֹלְטִין sholtin בּוֹ bo שֶׁנֶּאֱמַר shene'emar:

וְהָסֵר vehaser כַּעַס ka'as מִלִּבֶּךָ milibecha, וְהַעֲבֵר veha'aver רָעָה ra'a

מִבְּשָׂרֶךָ mibesarecha, וְאֵין ve'en רָעָה ra'a אֶלָּא ela גֵּיהִנָּם Gehinom,

שֶׁנֶּאֱמַר shene'emar: וְגַם־ vegam רָשָׁע rasha לְיוֹם leyom רָעָה ra'a.

"Hear, my son, the instruction of your father and don't forsake the teaching of your mother." (Proverbs 1:8). Get into the habit of always speaking calmly to everyone. This will prevent you from anger, a serious attribute flaw which causes people to sin. As our Teachers said: "Whoever flares up in anger is subject to the discipline of Gehinom" (Nedarim 22a) as it is said: "Cast out anger from your heart, and remove evil from your flesh." (Ecclesiastes 12:10) here Evil means Gehinom, as we read: "and the wicked are destined for the day of evil." (Proverbs 16:4)

וְכַאֲשֶׁר vecha'asher תִּנָּצֵל tinatzel מִן min הַכַּעַס haka'as תַּעֲלֶה ta'ale

עַל al לִבְּךָ libecha מִדַּת midat הָעֲנָוָה ha'anava שֶׁהִיא shehi מִדָּה mida

טוֹבָה tova מִכָּל mikol הַמִּדּוֹת hamidot טוֹבוֹת tovot, שֶׁנֶּאֱמַר shene'emar:

עֵקֶב ekev עֲנָוָה anava יִרְאַת yir'at יְהֹוָה Adonai וּבַעֲבוּר uva'avur

הָעֲנָוָה ha'anava תַּעֲלֶה ta'ale עַל al לִבְּךָ libecha מִדַּת midat הַיִּרְאָה hayir'a, כִּי ki

תִתֵּן titen אֶל el לִבְּךָ libecha תָּמִיד tamid, מֵאַיִן me'ayin בָּאתָ bata, וּלְאָן ul'an

אַתָּה ata הוֹלֵךְ holech, וְשֶׁאַתָּה veshe'ata רִמָּה rima וְתוֹלֵעָה vetole'a

בְּחַיֶּיךָ bechayecha, וְאַף ve'af כִּי ki בְּמוֹתָךְ vemotach, וְלִפְנֵי velifnei בְּמִי mi

אַתָּה ata עָתִיד atid לִיתֵּן liten דִּין din וְחֶשְׁבּוֹן vecheshbon, לִפְנֵי lifnei

מֶלֶךְ Melech הַכָּבוֹד haKavod, שֶׁנֶּאֱמַר shene'emar: הִנֵּה hine

הַשָּׁמַיִם hashamayim וּשְׁמֵי ushmei הַשָּׁמַיִם hashamayim לֹא lo

יְכַלְכְּלוּךָ yechalkelucha, אַף af כִּי ki לִבּוֹת libot בְּנֵי benei אָדָם adam,

וְנֶאֱמַר vene'emar: הֲלֹא halo אֶת־ et הַשָּׁמַיִם hashamayim וְאֶת־ ve'et

הָאָרֶץ ha'aretz אֲנִי Ani מָלֵא male נְאֻם־ ne'um יְהֹוָה Adonai

Once you have saved yourself from anger, the quality of humility will enter your heart. This radiant attribute is the finest of all admirable attributes (see Avoda Zara 20b), *"Following humility comes the fear (awe) of the Lord."* (Proverbs 22:4), *and through humility, the attribute of awe will enter your heart. It will cause you to always think about where you came from and where you are going, and that while alive you are only like a maggot and a worm, and the same after death. It will also remind you before Whom you will be judged, the King of Glory* (see Avot 3:1), *as it is written, "Even the heaven and the heavens of heaven can't contain You, How much less the hearts of people!"* (I Kings 8:27; Proverbs 15:11) *It is also written: "Do I not fill heaven and earth? says the Lord."* (Jeremiah 23:24)

וְכַאֲשֶׁר vecha'asher תַּחְשׁוֹב tachshov אֵת et כָּל kol אֵלֶּה ele, תִּירָא tira

מִבּוֹרַאֲךָ mibor'echa וְתִשָּׁמֵר vetishamer מִן min הַחֵטְא hachet, וּבְמִדּוֹת uvmidot

הָאֵלֶּה ha'ele תִּהְיֶה tih'ye שָׂמֵחַ same'ach בְּחֶלְקֶךָ bechelkecha.

וְכַאֲשֶׁר vecha'asher תִּתְנַהֵג titnaheg בְּמִדַּת bemidat הָעֲנָוָה ha'anava

לְהִתְבּוֹשֵׁשׁ lehitboshesh מִכָּל mikol אָדָם adam וּלְהִתְפַּחֵד ulhitpached

מִמֶּנּוּ mimenu וּמִן umin הַחֵטְא hachet, אָז az תִּשְׁרֶה tishre עָלֶיךָ alecha

רוּחַ ru'ach הַשְּׁכִינָה haShechina, וְזִיו veziv כְּבוֹדָה kevoda, וְחַיֵּי vechayei

עוֹלָם olam הַבָּא haba. וְעַתָּה ve'ata בְּנִי beni דַּע da וּרְאֵה ur'e, כִּי ki

הַמִּתְגָּאֶה hamitga'e בְּלִבּוֹ belibo עַל al הַבְּרִיּוֹת haberiyot, מוֹרֵד mored הוּא hu

בְּמַלְכוּת bemalchut שָׁמַיִם shamayim, כִּי ki מִתְפָּאֵר mitpa'er הוּא hu

בִּלְבוּשׁ bilvush מַלְכוּת malchut שָׁמַיִם shamayim, שֶׁנֶּאֱמַר shene'emar:

יְהֹוָה Adonai מָלָךְ malach גֵּאוּת ge'ut לָבֵשׁ lavesh וְגוֹ vegomer.

וּבַמֶּה uvame יִתְגָּאֶה yitga'e לֵב lev הָאָדָם ha'adam, אִם im

בְּעוֹשֶׁר be'osher, יְהֹוָה Adonai מוֹרִישׁ morish וּמַעֲשִׁיר uma'ashir.

When you think about all these things, you will come to fear Your creator, and you will protect yourself from sinning and therefore with these attributes you will be happy with your share. Also, when you act humbly and modestly before everyone, and are afraid of God and of sin, then the spirit of the Shechinah and its glorious radiance will rest upon you, and you will live the life of the World-to-Come! And now, my son, understand and see that whoever his heart proud and feels that he is greater than others is rebelling against the Kingdom of heaven, because he is adorning himself with the garments of the kingdom of heaven, as it is written: "The Lord reigns, He wears clothes of pride." (Psalm 93:1) Why should one's heart feel proud? Is it because of wealth? "The Lord makes one poor or rich." (1 Samuel 2:7)

וְאִם ve'im, בְּכָבוֹד bechavod, הֲלֹא halo, לָאֱלֹקִים lelokim, הוּא hu,

שֶׁנֶּאֱמַר: shene'emar, וְהָעֹשֶׁר veha'osher, וְהַכָּבוֹד vehakavod, מִלְּפָנֶיךָ milfanecha,

וְאֵיךְ ve'ech, מִתְפָּאֵר mitpa'er, בְּכָבוֹד bichvod, קוֹנוֹ kono. וְאִם ve'im

מִתְפָּאֵר mitpa'er, בְּחָכְמָה bechochma, מֵסִיר mesir, שָׂפָה safa

לְנֶאֱמָנִים lene'emanim, וְטַעַם veta'am, זְקֵנִים zekenim, יִקָּח yikach. נִמְצָא nimtza

הַכֹּל hakol, שָׁוֶה shave, לִפְנֵי lifnei, הַמָּקוֹם haMakom, כִּי ki, בְּאַפּוֹ ve'apo

מַשְׁפִּיל mashpil, גֵּאִים ge'im, וּבִרְצוֹנוֹ uvirtzono, מַגְבִּיהַּ magbiha, שְׁפָלִים shefalim,

לָכֵן lachen, הַשְׁפִּיל hashpil, עַצְמְךָ atzmecha, וִינַשֵּׂאֲךָ vinas'acha, הַמָּקוֹם haMakom.

עַל al כֵּן ken, אֲפָרֵשׁ afaresh, לְךָ lecha, אֵיךְ ech, תִּתְנַהֵג titnaheg, בְּמִדַּת bemidat

הָעֲנָוָה ha'anava, לָלֶכֶת lalechet, בָּהּ ba, תָּמִיד tamid, כָּל kol, דְּבָרֶיךָ devarecha

יִהְיוּ yih'yu, בְּנַחַת benachat, וְרֹאשְׁךָ veroshcha, כָּפוּף kafuf, וְעֵינֶיךָ ve'enecha,

יַבִּיטוּ yabitu, לְמַטָּה lemata, לָאָרֶץ la'aretz, וְלִבְּךָ velibecha, לְמַעְלָה lem'ala,

וְאַל ve'al, תַּבִּיט tabit, בִּפְנֵי bifnei, אָדָם adam, בְּדַבֶּרְךָ bedaberecha, עִמּוֹ imo.

Is it because of honor? It belongs to God, as we read: "Wealth and honor come from You." (1 Chronicles 29:12) So how could one adorn himself with his master's honor? And one who is proud of his wisdom surely knows that God "takes away the speech of assured men and reasoning from the sages." (Job 12:20) So we see that everyone is the same before God, since with His anger He lowers the proud and when he wishes He raises the low. So lower you and God will lift you up! Therefore, I will now explain to you how to behave humbly and always follow this attribute. Speak gently at all times, with your head bowed, your eyes looking down to the ground and your heart up (towards God). Don't look at a person's face while you speak to them.

וְכָל vechol אָדָם adam יִהְיֶה yih'ye גָּדוֹל gadol מִמְּךָ mimecha בְּעֵינֶיךָ be'enecha,

וְאִם ve'im וְחָכָם chacham אוֹ oh עָשִׁיר ashir הוּא hu, עָלֶיךָ alecha

לְכַבְּדוֹ lechabedo. וְאִם ve'im רָשׁ rash הוּא hu, וְאַתָּה ve'ata עָשִׁיר ashir אוֹ oh

וְחָכָם chacham מִמֶּנּוּ mimenu, וְחָשׁוּב chashov בְּלְבָבֶךָ belibecha כִּי ki אַתָּה ata

חַיָּב chayav מִמֶּנּוּ mimenu וְהוּא vehu זַכַּאי zakai מִמְּךָ mimach, שֶׁאִם she'im

הוּא hu חוֹטֵא chote הוּא הוּא hu שׁוֹגֵג shogeg וְאַתָּה ve'ata בְּמֵזִיד mezid. בְּכָל bechol

דְּבָרֶיךָ devarecha וּמַעֲשֶׂיךָ uma'asecha וּמַחְשְׁבוֹתֶיךָ umach'shevotecha

וּבְכָל uvchol עֵת et, וְחָשׁוּב chashov בְּלְבָבָךְ belibach כְּאִלוּ ke'ilu אַתָּה ata

עוֹמֵד omed לִפְנֵי lifnei קָדוֹשׁ Kadosh בָּרוּךְ Baruch הוּא Hu,

וּשְׁכִינָתוֹ uSh'chinato עָלֶיךָ alecha, כִּי ki כְּבוֹדוֹ kevodo מָלֵא male

הָעוֹלָם ha'olam, וּדְבָרֶיךָ udvarecha יִהְיוּ yih'yu בְּאֵימָה be'ema וּבְיִרְאָה uvyir'a

כְּעֶבֶד ke'eved לִפְנֵי lifnei רַבּוֹ rabo, וְתִתְבַּיֵּשׁ vetitbayesh מִכָּל mikol אָדָם adam,

וְאִם ve'im יִקְרָאֲךָ yikra'acha אִישׁ ish אַל al תַּעֲנֵהוּ ta'anehu בְּקוֹל bekol

רָם ram, רַק rak בְּנַחַת benachat כְּעוֹמֵד ke'omed לִפְנֵי lifnei רַבּוֹ rabo.

Consider everyone as greater than yourself. If he is wise or rich, you should give him respect. If he is poor and you are richer or wiser than he, consider yourself (in your heart) to be more guilty than he, and that he is more innocent than you, since when he sins it is err, while your sin is deliberate! In all your words, all your actions, all your thoughts and in any time regard yourself as standing before The Holy One Blessed Be He, and His Shechinah is above you, for His glory fills the whole world. Speak with fear and awe, as a slave standing before his master. Act with restraint in front of everyone. When someone calls you, don't answer loudly, but gently, as one who stands before his master.

vehevei וֶהֱוֵי zahir זָהִיר likrot לִקְרוֹת batorah בַּתּוֹרָה tamid תָּמִיד

asher אֲשֶׁר tuchal תּוּכַל lekayema לְקַיְּמָה, vecha'asher וְכַאֲשֶׁר takum תָּקוּם

min מִן hasefer הַסֵּפֶר, techapes תְּחַפֵּשׂ ba'asher בַּאֲשֶׁר lamadeta לָמַדְתָּ im אִם

yesh יֵשׁ bo בּוֹ davar דָּבָר asher אֲשֶׁר tuchal תּוּכַל lekayemo לְקַיְּמוֹ,

uvaze וּבְזֶה yih'yu יִהְיוּ kol כָּל yamecha יָמֶיךָ bit'shuva בִּתְשׁוּבָה.

vehaser וְהָסֵר kol כָּל divrei דִּבְרֵי ha'olam הָעוֹלָם milibecha מִלִּבְּךָ be'et בְּעֵת

hatefila הַתְּפִלָּה, vehachen וְהָכֵן libecha לִבְּךָ lifnei לִפְנֵי haMakom הַמָּקוֹם

Baruch בָּרוּךְ Hu הוּא, vetaher וְטַהֵר ra'yonecha רַעְיוֹנֶיךָ, vachashov וַחֲשׁוֹב

hadibur הַדִּבּוּר kodem קוֹדֶם shetotzi'enu שֶׁתּוֹצִיאֶנּוּ mipicha מִפִּיךָ,

vechen וְכֵן ta'ase תַּעֲשֶׂה kol כָּל yemei יְמֵי chayei חַיֵּי hevlecha הֶבְלֶךָ

bechol בְּכָל davar דָּבָר vedavar וְדָבָר velo וְלֹא techeta תֶחֱטָא.

Torah should always be learned diligently, so you will be able to fulfill its commands. When you arise from your learning reflect carefully on what you have studied, in order to see what in it you can put into practice. Examine your actions every morning and evening, and in this way every one of your days will be spent in Teshuvah (repentance). During your prayers, remove all worldly concerns from your heart. Prepare your heart before the Lord, purify your thoughts and think about what you are going to say before saying it. If you follow this in all your daily actions, you will not come to sin.

uvaze וּבְזֶה | yih'yu יִהְיוּ | devarecha דְּבָרֶיךָ | uma'asecha וּמַעֲשֶׂיךָ

umachshevotecha וּמַחְשְׁבוֹתֶיךָ | yesharim יְשָׁרִים, | utfilatcha וּתְפִלָּתְךָ

tih'ye תִּהְיֶה | zaka זַכָּה | uvara וּבָרָה | unkiya וּנְקִיָּה | umechuvenet וּמְכֻוֶּנֶת

umekubelet וּמְקֻבֶּלֶת | lifnei לִפְנֵי | haMakom הַמָּקוֹם | Baruch בָּרוּךְ | Hu הוּא,

shene'emar שֶׁנֶּאֱמַר: | tachin תָּכִין | libam לִבָּם | takshiv תַּקְשִׁיב | oznecha אָזְנֶךָ.

tikra תִּקְרָא | ha'igeret הָאִגֶּרֶת | hazot הַזֹּאת | pa'am פַּעַם | achat אַחַת

bashavu'a בַּשָּׁבוּעַ | velo וְלֹא | tifchot תִּפְחוֹת, | lekayema לְקַיְּמָה, | velalechet וְלָלֶכֶת

ba בָּה | tamid תָּמִיד | achar אַחַר | hashem הַשֵּׁם | yitbarech יִתְבָּרֵךְ,

lema'an לְמַעַן | tatzli'ach תַּצְלִיחַ | bechol בְּכָל | derachecha דְּרָכֶיךָ | vetizke וְתִזְכֶּה

la'olam לָעוֹלָם | haba הַבָּא | hatzafun הַצָּפוּן | latzadikim לַצַּדִּיקִים.

uvchol וּבְכָל | yom יוֹם | shetikra'ena שֶׁתִּקְרָאֶנָּה | ya'anucha יַעֲנוּךָ | min מִן

hashamayim הַשָּׁמַיִם | ka'asher כַּאֲשֶׁר | ya'ale יַעֲלֶה | al עַל | libecha לִבֶּךָ

lish'ol לִשְׁאוֹל | ad עַד | olam עוֹלָם | amen אָמֵן | sela סֶלָה:

This way everything you say, do or think will be proper, and your prayer will be pure, clear, clean, devout and acceptable before the Lord blessed Be He, as it is written: "When their heart is directed to You, listen to them." (Psalms 10:17) *Read this letter at least once a week and neglect none of it. Fulfill it, and in so doing, walk with it forever in the ways of the Lord, may He Be Blessed, so that you will succeed in all your ways, and merit the World to Come which lies hidden away for the righteous. Every day that you shall read this letter, heaven shall answer your heart's desires eternally. Amen, Sela.*

Petichat Eliyahu – The Opening of Elijah the Prophet

Reciting these paragraphs can help you open your heart to spiritual wisdom.

alenu עָלֵינוּ ילה Elohenu אֱלֹהֵינוּ ללה Adonai אֲדֹנָי no'am נֹעַם vihi וִיהִי

alenu עָלֵינוּ konena כּוֹנְנָה yadenu יָדֵינוּ uma'ase וּמַעֲשֵׂה

konenehu כּוֹנְנֵהוּ yadenu יָדֵינוּ uma'ase וּמַעֲשֵׂה

hanavi הַנָּבִיא לכב Eliyahu אֵלִיָּהוּ patach פָּתַח,

zachur זָכוּר ע"ב קס"א, יהי אור ע"ה (סוד המשכת השפע מן ד' שמות ליסוד הנקרא זכור)

letov לְטוֹב והו ; זכור לטוב = בוזוחר, סנדלפון, ערי ; אליהו הנביא זכור לטוב = ת' כנגד ת' כוזוות הס"א

de'ant דְּאַנְתְּ almin עָלְמִין מ"ה ב"ן ס"ג ע"ב יהוה ribon רִבּוֹן ve'amar וְאָמַר:

hu הוּא ant אַנְתְּ bechushban בְּוֹשְׁבָּן, vela וְלֹא chad וַד hu הוּא

al עַל setima סְתִימָא ila'in עִלָּאִין ; עמם ילי kol כֹּל al עַל ila'a עִלָּאָה

tefisa תְּפִיסָא machashava בְּוֹוֹשָׁבָה let לֵית, setimin סְתִימִין ; עמם ילי kol כֹּל

eser עֲשֵׂר de'apakt דְּאַפֵּקְתְּ hu הוּא ant אַנְתְּ kelal כְּלָל bach בָּךְ

sefiran סְפִירָן, eser עֲשֵׂר lon כּוֹן vekarenan וְקָרֵינָן, tikunin תִּקּוּנִין

"And may the pleasantness of the Lord, our God, be upon us and may He establish the work of our hands for us and may the work of our hands establish Him" (Psalms 90:17). Elijah opened, saying: Master of the worlds, You are One without enumeration. You are above all high ones, the most concealed of all. No thought can grasp You at all. You are the one that produced the ten emanations. And we named them ten Sefirot,

dela דְּלָא setimin סְתִימִין almin עָלְמִין behon בְּהוֹן le'anhaga לְאַנְהָגָא

uv'hon וּבְהוֹן ◆de'itgalyan דְּאִתְגַּלְיָן ve'almin וְעָלְמִין itgalyan אִתְגַּלְיָן

hu הוּא ve'ant וְאַנְתְּ ◆nasha נָשָׁא mibenei מִבְּנֵי itkasi'at אִתְכַּסִּיאַת

de'ant דְּאַנְתְּ uvgin וּבְגִין ◆lon לוֹן umyached וּמְיַחֵד lon לוֹן dekashir דְּקָשִׁיר

min בִּן chad וָזֹד de'afrish דְּאַפְרִישׁ man מָאן kol כָּל milgav מִלְגָאו

lei לֵיהּ itchashiv אִתְחַשִׁיב ,eser עֶשֶׂר me'ilen מֵאִלֵּין chavrei וְחַבְרֵיהּ

sefiran סְפִירָן eser עֶשֶׂר ve'ilen וְאִלֵּין ◆bach בָּךְ afrish אַפְרִישׁ ke'ilu כְּאִלּוּ

vechad וְוָזֹד ,arich אָרִיךְ chad וָזֹד ,kesidran כְּסִדְרָן azlin אַזְלִין inun אִינּוּן

hu הוּא ve'ant וְאַנְתְּ ◆benoni בֵּינוֹנִי vechad וְוָזֹד ,katzer קָצֵר

◆lach לָךְ de'anhig דְּאַנְהִיג man מָאן velet וְלֵית ,lon לוֹן de'anhig דְּאַנְהִיג

◆mikol מִכָּל vela וְלָא ,letata לְתַתָּא vela וְלָא ,le'ela לְעֵילָא la לָא

deminayhu דִּמְנַּיְהוּ ,lon לוֹן takant תַּקָּנַת levushin לְבוּשִׁין ◆sitra סִטְרָא

◆nasha נָשָׁא livnei לִבְנֵי nishmatin נִשְׁמָתִין farchin פַּרְחִין

to conduct with them obscure worlds that are not revealed, and revealed worlds. And through them, You are screened from human beings. And You are the One who connects them and unites them. And because you are from within, thus, anyone who separates these ten one from the other, to give dominance to that one alone, it is considered for him, as if he separates in You. And these ten Sefirot follow their order, the one is long, and one, is short. And the one is average. And You conduct them, and there is no other who will lead You, neither Above, nor Below, nor in any other side. You prepared garments, from which the Neshamot fly to the human beings and you prepared several bodies.

de'itkeri'u דְּאִתְקְרִיאוּ, לוֹן lon תַּקָּנַת takant גּוּפִין gufin וְכַמָּה vechama

דְּמִכַסְיָן dim'chasyan לְבוּשִׁין levushin לְגַבֵּי legabei גּוּפָא gufa

דָּא da, בְּתִקּוּנָא betikuna וְאִתְקְרִיאוּ ve'itkeri'u עֲלֵיהוֹן alehon.

וְחֶסֶד Chesed ע"ב, ריבוע יהוה דְּרוֹעָא dero'a יְמִינָא yemina, גְּבוּרָה Gevurah רי"ו

דְּרוֹעָא dero'a שְׂמָאלָא semala, תִּפְאֶרֶת Tiferet גּוּפָא gufa, נֶצַח Netzach

וְהוֹד veHod ההה תְּרֵין teren שׁוֹקִין shokin, יְסוֹד Yesod ההע סִיּוּמָא siyuma

דְּגוּפָא degufa אוֹת ot בְּרִית berit קֹדֶשׁ kodesh, מַלְכוּת Malchut פֶּה pe

שֶׁבְּעַל shebe'al פֶּה pe מילה ; וע"ה אלהים, אהיה אדני תּוֹרָה torah. מילה ; וע"ה אלהים,

קָרֵינָן karenan לָהּ la. וְחָכְמָה Chochmah במילוי = תרי"ג (מצוות) אהיה אדני

מִלְגָּאו milgav, מַחֲשָׁבָה mach'shava אִיהוּ ihu, מוֹחָא mocha,

בִּינָה Binah ע"ה וזיים, אהיה אהיה יהוה לִבָּא liba לְבָא uva וּבַהּ

הַלֵב halev מֵבִין mevin וְעַל ve'al אִלֵּין ilen תְּרֵין teren

כְּתִיב ketiv: הַנִּסְתָּרֹת hanistarot לַיהֹוָה ladonai (ואהדי אהדונהי) לְיְהֹוָ"ה Elohenu אֱלֹהֵינוּ יכה

And they are named bodies in relation to the clothing, in which they are attired.
The Sefirot are named by this emendation, Chesed being the right arm, Gevurah being the left arm.
Tiferet means the body. Netzach and Hod, the two thighs, Yesod the final part of the body,
the sign of the Holy Covenant, Malchut, the mouth, we call it the Oral Torah.
Chochmah is the brain, the thought within. Binah is the heart, and through it, the heart understands.
And about these two, it is written, "The secret things belong to the Lord our God" (Deuteronomy 29:28).

כֶּתֶר Keter יהוה מלך יהוה מלך יהוה ימלוך לעולם ועד (באתב"ש גאל), עֶלְיוֹן elyon, אִיהוּ ihu

כֶּתֶר keter יהוה מלך יהוה מלך יהוה ימלוך לעולם ועד (באתב"ש גאל) מַלְכוּת malchut◆

וְעָלֵיהּ ve'alei פהל :אִתְּמַר itmar מַגִּיד magid מֵרֵאשִׁית mereshit

אַחֲרִית acharit◆ וְאִיהוּ ve'ihu קַרְקַפְתָּא karkafta דִּתְפִלֵּי ditfilei◆

מִלְגָּאו milgav אִיהוּ ihu אוֹת ot יוּ"ד Yud וְאוֹת ve'ot ה"א He וְאוֹת ve'ot

וָא"ו Vav וְאוֹת ve'ot ה"א He, דְּאִיהוּ de'ihu אֲרֹחַ orach אֲצִילוּת atzilut,

אִיהוּ ihu שַׁקְיוּ shakyu דְּאִילָנָא de'ilana בִּדְרוֹעֵוי bidro'oy וְעַנְפוֹי ve'anpoy,

כְּמַיָּא kemaya דְּאַשְׁקֵי de'ashkei לְאִילָנָא le'ilana וְאִתְרַבֵּי ve'itrabei

בְּהַהוּא behahu שַׁקְיוּ shakyu◆ רִבּוֹן ribon יהוה ע"ב ס"ג מ"ה ב"ן עָלְמִין almin,

אַנְתְּ ant הוּא hu עִלַּת ilat הָעִלּוֹת ha'ilot, וְסִבַּת vesibat הַסִּבּוֹת hasibot,

דְּאַשְׁקֵי de'ashkei לְאִילָנָא le'ilana בְּהַהוּא behahu נְבִיעוּ nevi'u,

וְהַהוּא vehahu נְבִיעוּ nevi'u אִיהוּ ihu כְּנִשְׁמָתָא kenishmeta לְגוּפָא legufa,

דְּאִיהִי de'ihi וְחַיִּים chayim אהיה יהוה, בינה אהיה ע"ה לְגוּפָא legufa◆

The Supernal Keter is the crown of Malchut. And about this is said, "Declaring the end from the beginning" (Isaiah 46:10). And that is the skull of the Tefilin. Within is Yud-Vav-Dalet, Hei- Alef, Vav-Alef-Vav, Hei-Alef, which is in the path of Atzilut. It is the watering of the tree in its arms and branches, as waters that water that tree and it multiplies by this watering. Master of the Worlds, You are the Cause of all Causes, and the Reason for all Reasons, that waters the tree by that stream, and that spring is like a soul to the body, that is the life of the body.

,diyukna דְּיוּקְנָא velet וְלֵית ,dimyon דְּמְיוֹן let לֵית uvach וּבָךְ

ulvar וּלְבַר dilgav דִּלְגָאו מ"ה ma מַה ילי mikol מִכָּל

ve'apakt וְאַפֵּקְתְּ ,ve'ar'a וְאַרְעָא shemaya שְׁמַיָא uvarata וּבָרָאתָ

vechochvaya וְכֹכְבַיָא vesihara וְסִיהֲרָא shimsha שִׁמְשָׁא minehon מִנְּהוֹן

udsha'in וּדְשָׁאִין ilanin אִלָנִין ,uve'ar'a וּבְאַרְעָא umazalei וּמַזָּלֵי

vechevan וְחֵיוָן ve'isbin וְעִשְׂבִּין de'eden דְּעֵדֶן veginta וְגִנְתָא

nasha נָשָׁא uvnei וּבְנֵי uv'irin וּבְעִירִין venunin וְנוּנִין ve'ofin וְעוֹפִין

ila'in עִלָאִין behon בְּהוֹן le'ishtemode'a לְאִשְׁתְּמוֹדְעָא

vetata'in וְתַתָּאִין ila'in עִלָאִין behon בְּהוֹן yitnahagun יִתְנַהֲגוּן ve'ech וְאֵיךְ

vetata'ei וְתַתָּאֵי me'ila'ei מֵעִלָאֵי ishtemode'an אִשְׁתְּמוֹדְעָן ve'ech וְאֵיךְ

יצחק, ד"פ ב"ן uvar וּבַר ,kelal כְּלָל bach בָּךְ deyada דְּיָדַע velet וְלֵית

,vetata'ei וְתַתָּאֵי be'ila'ei בְּעִלָאֵי yichuda יְחוּדָא let לֵית minach מִנָּךְ

kola כֹּלָא al עַל אני adon אֲדוֹן ishtemoda אִשְׁתְּמוֹדַע ve'ant וְאַנְתְּ

And to Yourself there is no likeness nor form inside or outside. And You created heavens
and earth and produced from them sun and moon and stars and constellations. And in the earth,
trees and grasses, and the Garden of Eden, and plants, and animals and fowl and fish
and human beings, through them to acknowledge the high ones, and how the higher
and lower ones behave. And how the lower ones recognize to attain from the higher ones;
and in you, there is absolutely nobody who is knowledgeable. And besides your unification,
there is no such unique unity in the upper and lower ones, and You are recognized as the Master over all.

וְכָל vechol סְפִירָן sefiran, כָּל kol וְחַד chad אִית it לֵיהּ lei שֵׁם shem

יְדִיעַ yedi'a, וּבְהוֹן uvhon אִתְקְרִיאוּ itkeri'u מַלְאֲכַיָּא mal'achaya.

וְאַנְתְּ ve'ant לֵית let כָּךְ lach שֵׁם shem יְדִיעַ yedi'a, דְּאַנְתְּ de'ant הוּא hu

מְמַלֵּא memale כָּל kol יְלֵי שְׁמָהָן shemahan, וְאַנְתְּ ve'ant הוּא hu

שְׁלִימוּ shelimu דְּכֻלְּהוּ dechulhu, וְכַד vechad אַנְתְּ ant תִּסְתַּלַּק tistalak

מִנְּהוֹן minehon אִשְׁתָּאֲרוּ ishte'aru כֻּלְּהוּ kulehu שְׁמָהָן shemahan

כְּגוּפָא kegufa בְּלָא bela נִשְׁמָתָא nishmata. אַנְתְּ ant וְזַכִּים chakim

וְלָאו velav בְּחָכְמָה beChochmah (במילוי = תרי"ג (מצוות)) יְדִיעָא yedi'a. אַנְתְּ ant

הוּא hu מֵבִין mevin, וְלָאו velav מִבִּינָה miBinah (ע"ה וזיים, אהיה יהוה)

יְדִיעָא yedi'a. לֵית let כָּךְ lach אֲתַר atar יְדִיעָא yedi'a.

אֶלָּא ela לְאִשְׁתְּמוֹדְעָא le'ishtemode'a תְּקְפָּךְ tukfach

וְזֵילָךְ vechelach לִבְנֵי livnei נָשָׁא nasha, וּלְאַחֲזָאָה ule'achza'a

לוֹן lon, אֵיךְ ech אִתְנְהִיג itnehig עָלְמָא alma בְּדִינָא vedina

וּבְרַחֲמֵי uvrachamei, דְּאִינוּן de'inun צֶדֶק tzedek וּמִשְׁפַּט umishpat

(ע"ה ה"פ אלהים) כְּפוּם kefum עוֹבָדֵיהוֹן ovadehon דִּבְנֵי divnei נָשָׁא nasha.

Each of the Sefirot has a recognizable name, of its own. And by them the angels are named. Yet you have no known name, You are He, who fills all the names. And it is You who completes them all. And when You are gone from them, all the names remain as body without a soul. You are wise, but not with known wisdom. You understand, but not with any known understanding. And You do not occupy any known place so that human beings should perceive His strength and might and to show them how the world conducted with justice and mercy that are righteousness and just trial, according to the deeds of the lower ones.

דִּין, din · אִיהוּ ihu · גְּבוּרָה gevurah · רי"ו · מִשְׁפָּט mishpat · ע"ה ה"פ אלהים

עֲמוּדָא amuda · דְּאֶמְצָעִיתָא de'emtza'ita · צֶדֶק tzedek, מַלְכוּתָא malchuta

קַדִּישָׁא kadisha · מֹאזְנֵי moznei · צֶדֶק tzedek, תְּרֵין teren · סַמְכֵי samchei · kula

קְשׁוֹט keshot · הִין hin · צֶדֶק, tzedek · אוֹת ot · בְּרִית berit · כְּלָא kula

לְאַחְזָאָה le'achza'a · אֵיךְ ech · אִתְנְהִיג itnehig · עָלְמָא alma

אֲבָל aval · לָאו lav · דְּאִית de'it · לָךְ lach · צֶדֶק tzedek · יְדִיעָא yedi'a

דְּאִיהוּ de'ihu · דִּין, din · וְלָאו velav · מִשְׁפָּט mishpat ע"ה ה"פ אלהים · יְדִיעָא yedi'a

דְּאִיהוּ de'ihu · רַחֲמֵי, rachamei · וְלָאו velav · מִכָּל mikol · יל" · אִלֵּין ilen

מִדּוֹת midot · כְּלָל kelal · קוּם kum · רִבִּי Ribi · שִׁמְעוֹן Shimon

וְיִתְחַדְּשׁוּן veyitchadeshun · מִלִּין milin · עַל al · יְדָךְ, yedach · דְּהָא deha

רְשׁוּתָא reshuta · אִית it · לָךְ lach · לְגַלָּאָה legala'a · רָזִין razin · טְמִירִין temirin

עַל al · יְדָךְ yedach · בַּה ma · דְּלָא dela · אִתְיְהִיב ityehiv · רְשׁוּ reshu

לְגַלָּאָה legala'a · לְשׁוּם leshum · בַּר bar · נָשׁ nash · עַד ad · כְּעַן ke'an

Judgement is Gevurah, judicial trial is the Central Column, Righteousness - the holy Malchut; just scales are two supports of truth. A truly measured hin is this sign of the covenant of Yesod. All to show the leadership of the world, but it is not as if there is certain justice that is strictly judgmental, and not a certain just trial that is strictly of mercy, and or of any of these attributes, at all. Rise, Rabbi Shimon and let new ideas come through you, as you have permission, that through you obscure mysteries will be revealed, because permission was not granted to any person until now to reveal them.

kam קָם Ribi רִבִּי Shim'on שִׁמְעוֹן, patach פָּתַח, ve'amar וְאָמַר: lecha לָךְ

Adonai יְהֹוָה(אלהים־אהדונהי) haGedula הַגְּדֻלָּה vehaGevurah וְהַגְּבוּרָה רי"ו

vehaTiferet וְהִתְפָּאֶרֶת vehaNetzach וְהַנֶּצַח vehaHod וְהַהוֹד ההה

ki כִּי chol כֹּל בַּשָּׁמַיִם bashamayim ilu וּבָאָרֶץ uva'aretz

lecha לָךְ Adonai יְהֹוָה(אלהים־אהדונהי) hamamlacha הַמַּמְלָכָה vegomer וְגוֹ׳,

inun אִינוּן, shema'u שִׁמְעוּ ila'in עִלָּאִין, (Here, you should give three coins to charity)

demichin דְּמִיכִין deChevron דְּחֶבְרוֹן veRaya וְרַעְיָא מְהֵימְנָא Mehemna,

it'aru אִתְעָרוּ mishenatchon מִשֵּׁנַתְכוֹן, hakitzu הָקִיצוּ veranenu וְרַנְּנוּ

shochnei שֹׁכְנֵי afar עָפָר, ilen אִלֵּין inun אִינוּן tzadikaya צַדִּיקַיָּא,

de'inun דְּאִנּוּן misitra מִסִּטְרָא dehahu דְּהַהוּא de'itmar דְּאִתְּמַר ba בֵּהּ:

ani אֲנִי yeshena יְשֵׁנָה velibi וְלִבִּי er עֵר, velav וְלָאו inun אִינוּן

metim מֵתִים, uvgin וּבְגִין da דָּא itmar אִתְּמַר vehon בְּהוֹן hakitzu הָקִיצוּ

veranenu וְרַנְּנוּ vegomer וְגוֹ׳, Raya רַעְיָא Mehemna מְהֵימְנָא, ant אַנְתְּ

va'avahan וְאַבָהָן, hakitzu הָקִיצוּ veranenu וְרַנְּנוּ le'it'aruta לְאִתְעָרוּתָא

dish'chinta דִּשְׁכִינְתָּא de'ihi דְּאִיהִי yeshena יְשֵׁנָה vegaluta בְּגָלוּתָא

Rabbi Shimon rose, opened and said, "Yours, Lord, is the greatness, and the power..."
(1 Chronicles 29:11). Listen, Supreme Ones, they who rest in Chevron, and the Faithful Shepherd,
be shaken off from your sleep. "Awake and sing, you that dwell in dust" (Isaiah 26:19). It is those righteous
that are from this aspect about which is said, "I sleep, but my heart wakes" (Song of Songs 5:2).
And they are not dead, therefore it says about them, "Awake and sing..." Faithful Shepherd,
you and the Patriarchs, awake and sing to the waking of the Shechinah that sleeps in exile

דְּעַד de'ad | כְּעַן ke'an | צַדִּיקַיָּא tzadikaya | כֻּלְּהוּ kulhu | דְּמִיכִין demichin

וְשֵׁינְתָא veshinta | בְּחוֹרֵיהוֹן vechorehon ♦ | מִיַּד miyad | יְהִיבַת yahivat

שְׁכִינְתָּא shechinta | תְּלַת telat | קָלִין kalin | לְגַבֵּי legabei | רַעְיָא Raya

מְהֵימְנָא Meheimna | וְיֵימָא veyima | לֵיהּ lei | קוּם kum | רַעְיָא Raya

מְהֵימְנָא Mehemna, | דְּהָא deha | עֲלָךְ alach | אִתְּמַר itmar | קוֹל kol |

דּוֹדִי dodi | דּוֹפֵק dofek בוק | לְגַבַּאי legabai, | בְּאַרְבַּע be'arba | אַתְוָן atvan

דִּילֵיהּ dilei ♦ | וְיֵימָא veyima | בְּהוֹן vehon | פִּתְחִי pitchi | לִי li | אֲחוֹתִי achoti

רַעְיָתִי rayati | יוֹנָתִי yonati | תַּמָּתִי tamati ♦ | דְּהָא deha | תַּם tam | עֲוֹנֵךְ avonech

בַּת bat | צִיּוֹן Tziyon יוסף, ו הויות, קנאה | לֹא lo | יוֹסִיף yosif | לְהַגְלוֹתֵךְ lehaglotech ♦

שֵׁרֹאשִׁי sheroshi | נִמְלָא nimla | טַל tal יוד הא ואו, כוזו | נִמְלָא nimla | מַאי mai | נִמְלָא nimla

טַל tal יוד הא ואו, כוזו ♦ | אֶלָּא ela | אָמַר amar | קֻדְשָׁא kudsha | בְּרִיךְ berich

הוּא hu, | אַנְתְּ ant | וְשֶׁבַת chashavt | דְּמִיּוֹמָא demiyoma

דְּאִתְחֲרַב de'itcharav | בֵּי bei | מַקְדְּשָׁא makdesha | דְּעָאלְנָא de'alna

בְּבֵיתָא beveta | דִּילִי dili | וְעָאלְנָא ve'alna | בְּיִשּׁוּבָא veyishuva,

as up to now all the righteous are sleeping, and the sleep is in the caverns. Instantly, the Shechinah emits three sounds towards the Faithful Shepherd, and says to him 'Rise, faithful Shepherd. As about you it was said, "hark, my beloved is knocking" (Ibid.) by me, with His four letters. And he will say with them, "Open to me, my sister, my love, my dove, my undefiled" (Ibid.). Since, "The punishment of your iniquity is accomplished, daughter of Zion; he will no more carry you away into exile" (Lamentations 4:22). "For my head is filled with dew" (Song of Songs 5:2). He asks, "What is that which means 'Filled with dew'? But the Holy One, blessed be He, said, You think that from the day of the Temple's destruction, I entered My own abode, and I entered the settlement?

זִמְנָא zimna יכי כָּל kol עָאלְנָא alna דְּלָא dela, הֲכִי hachi לָאו lav

סִימָנָא simana כָּךְ lach הֲרֵי harei בְּגָלוּתָא begaluta, דְּאַנְתְּ de'ant

הֵ"א He,א כוזו., ואו, הא יוד טַל tal נִמְלָא nimla שֵׁרֹאשִׁי sheroshi

דִּילָהּ dila שְׁלִימוּ shelimu, בְּגָלוּתָא begaluta שְׁכִינְתָּא shechinta

וְזַיִּים vechayim אהיה אהיה יהוה, בינה ע"ה דִּילָהּ dila, אִיהוּ ihu טַל tal יוד הא ואו,

וְדָא veda אִיהוּ ihu אוֹת ot יוֹ"ד Yod וְאוֹת ve'ot הֵ"א He וְאוֹת ve'ot כוזו.

דְּלָא dela, שְׁכִינְתָּא shechinta אִיהִי ihi הֵ"א He וְאוֹת ve'ot וָא"ו Vav

הֵ"א He יוֹ"ד Yod אֶלָּא ela כוזו., ואו, הא יוד טַ"ל tal מְחֻשְׁבָּן mechushban

וָא"ו Vav, דְּסָלִיקוּ disliku אַתְוָון atvan לְוֹשְׁבָּן lechushban טַ"ל tal יוד הא ואו,

מִנְבִיעוּ minevi'u, לִשְׁכִינְתָּא lishchinta מַלְיָא malya דְּאִיהוּ de'ihu כוזו.

קָם kam מִיָּד miyad עִלָּאִין ilai'n מְקוֹרִין mekorin יכי דְּכָל dechol

קַדִּישִׁין kadishin וַאֲבָהָן va'avahan, מְהֵימְנָא Mehemna רַעְיָא Raya

דְּיִחוּדָא deyichuda רָזָא raza כָּאן kan עַד ad עִמֵּיהּ imei

Not so, as I have not entered as you are in exile. And here is your proof, "For my head is filled with dew". Hei-Alef is the Shechinah, and she is in exile. Her perfection, and her life is dew (Heb. tal = 39), and that is Yud-Vav-Dalet, Hei-Alef, Vav-Alef-Vav numerically tal (= 39). And the Hei-Alef, the Shechinah, was not in the reckoning of tal, only the Yud-Vav-Dalet, Hei-Alef, Vav-Alef-Vav, which amount to tal. And it is He, who fills the Shechinah from the fountain of all the Supernal sources. The Faithful Shepherd immediately rose up, and the holy Patriarchs with him. Up to here the mysteries of unification

בָּרוּךְ baruch יְהֹוָ֒אדני‎ Adonai לְעוֹלָם le'olam רִיבּוּעַ דס"ג וי' אותיות דס"ג

אָמֵן amen יאהדונהי וְאָמֵן ve'amen יאהדונהי ; ר"ת ; לאו:

וִיהֵא veyehe רַעֲוָא ra'ava מִן min קָדֶם kodam עַתִּיקָא atika

קַדִּישָׁא kadisha דְּכָל dechol ילי קַדִּישִׁין kadishin טְמִירָא temira

דְּכָל dechol ילי טְמִירִין temirin סְתִימָא setima דְּכֹלָּא dechola,

דְּיִתְמְשַׁךְ deyitmeshach טַלָּא tala עִילָּאָה ila'a מִנֵּיהּ minei לְמַלְיָא lemalya

רֵישֵׁיהּ reshei דִּזְעֵיר dize'ir אַנְפִּין anpin וּלְהַטִּיל ulehatil לַחֲקַל lachakal

תַּפּוּחִין tapuchin (שמו של מציון) אהיה יהוה אדני, מנוזם קַדִּישִׁין kadishin

בִּנְהִירוּ binhiru דְּאַנְפִּין de'anpin בְּרַעֲוָא bera'ava וּבְחֶדְוָתָא ubchedvata

דְּכֹלָּא dechola. וְיִתְמְשַׁךְ veyitmeshach מִן min קָדֶם kodam עַתִּיקָא atika

קַדִּישָׁא kadisha דְּכָל dechol ילי קַדִּישִׁין kadishin טְמִירָא temira

דְּכֹל dechol ילי טְמִירִין temirin סְתִימָא setima דְּכֹלָּא dechola.

וְיִתְמְשַׁךְ veyitmeshach מִן min קָדֶם kodam עַתִּיקָא atika קַדִּישָׁא kadisha

דְּכֹל dechol ילי קַדִּישִׁין kadishin טְמִירָא temira

דְּכֹל dechol ילי טְמִירִין temirin סְתִימָא setima דְּכֹלָּא dechola.

"Blessed be the Lord forever, Amen and Amen!" (Psalms 89:53) *And may it be pleasing before the holy of holiest Atika, the hidden of all and the most concealed, that a supernal dew will be drawn from him to fulfill the head of Zeir Anpin,and to drop to Chakal Tapuchin Kadishin from this shining face with desire and happiness for all. And also will be drawn from the holy of holiest Atika, the hidden of all and the most concealed*

re'uta רְעוּתָא verachamei וְרַחֲמֵי china וְחִנָּא vechisda וְחִסְדָּא

binhiru בִּנְהִירוּ ila'a עִלָּאָה bire'uta בִּרְעוּתָא vechedva וְחֶדְוָה

alai עֲלַי ve'al וְעַל kol כָּל ; עמם ילי benei בְּנֵי veti בֵּיתִי ב"פ ראה ve'al וְעַל

kol כָּל ; ילי עמם benei בְּנֵי Yisrael יִשְׂרָאֵל amei עַמֵּיה

veyifrekinan וְיִפְרְקִינָן mikol מִכָּל ילי aktin עָקְתִּין bishin בִּישִׁין

deyetun דְּיֵיתוּן le'alma לְעָלְמָא veyazmin וְיַזְמִין veyityehiv וְיִתְיְהִיב

lana לָנָא ulchol וּלְכָל יה ארני nafshatana נַפְשָׁתָנָא china וְחִנָּא

vechisda וְחִסְדָּא vechayei וְחַיֵּי arichei אֲרִיכֵי umzonei וּמְזוֹנֵי revichei רְוִיחֵי

verachamei וְרַחֲמֵי min מִן kodamei קֳדָמֵיה amen אָמֵן יאהדונהי

ken כֵּן yehi יְהִי ratzon רָצוֹן מהש ע"ה, ע"ב, בריבוע וקס"א ע"ה, אל שדי ע"ה

amen אָמֵן יאהדונהי ve'amen וְאָמֵן יאהדונהי

willingly, mercy, grace, kindness, with supernal illumination with desire and happiness, for me and for my household, and for all of Your people, Yisrael. And he will save us from all negative incidents that exist in our world. And he will bring and give us and all the rest of the people, grace and kindness, long life and sustenance, welfare and mercy from before him. Amen shall it be. Amen and Amen.

According to the wisdom of Kabbalah, spiritual purification allows us to connect to the highest levels of Divine Energy and Light. Every time we behave in a reactive and negative manner, we build another layer of darkness around ourselves. These layers are called *klipot* ("shells") and they separate us from the Light. Removal of these negative shells covering our soul brings about the spiritual purification of our body. Our personal healing, enlightenment, and good fortune increase in equal measure to the amount of purification we achieve. For that reason, the ancient sages advocated the use of a powerful and profound purification tool — *mikveh*, or immersion.

A *mikveh* is a pool of living waters. The waters in The Kabbalah Centre *mikveh* are living waters, sourced from underground wells. It is said that all the wells on Earth are interconnected.

Water is the physical expression of the Light of the Creator. It possesses truly magical qualities. Kabbalah teaches that water holds the keys to healing, longevity, regeneration, and even immortality.

Thus, when we dip ourselves in the *mikveh*, we are immersing our body and soul into the same pristine waters that flowed into the *mikveh* of Rav Isaac Luria. We are also connecting to the same holy waters of the Shiloach in Jerusalem, which were used by the high priests of the Temple over a thousand years ago.

The positive charge of the *mikveh* eliminates up to 400 levels of negativity. According to the technology of Kabbalah, the size of a *mikveh* must be forty *se'ah* (*se'ah* is an ancient measurement equal to the size of 144 eggs). Each *se'ah* helps us to purify ten levels of negativity (40 x 10 = 400 levels of negativity). The mikveh can counteract the forces of death by imbuing us with the primordial power of life. Spiritual blockages are cleansed as healing flows throughout our being.

The kabbalists recommend that we should immerse ourselves in a *mikveh* as often as possible.

We should immerse ourselves 11 times under the water. The first immersion activates the process of removing all the negativity. So before the first immersion we recite the following:

oyvecha אֹיְבֶיךָ veyafutzu וְיָפֻצוּ Adonai יְהֹוָאדֹנָיאהדונהי | (מקוה) קנ״א kuma קוּמָה

mipanecha מִפָּנֶיךָ mesan'echa מְשַׂנְאֶיךָ veyanusu וְיָנֻסוּ

ב״ן מ״ה ס״ג

Arise, Lord. Let Your enemies be scattered and let those who hate You flee before You.

Meditate to be surrounded by the Light of *Chasadim* (mercy) in order to destroy the impure system.

Recite the first verse of the *Ana Beko'ach*.

Chesed *(Alef Bet Gimel Yud Tav Tzadik)* אבג יתץ

◆yeminecha יְמִינֶךָ gedulat גְּדֻלַּת ◆beko'ach בְּכֹחַ ana אָנָּא

‡tzerura צְרוּרָה tatir תַּתִּיר

We beseech You, with the power of Your great right, undo this entanglement

Meditate on the following combinations from the 72 Names of God and *Ana Beko'ach* to connect to the energy of the *mikveh* and elevate the sparks of Light from the *Klipot*.

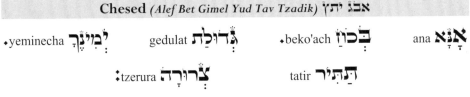

Recite the second verse of the *Ana Beko'ach* and meditate to shut down the reactive system:

Gevurah *(Kuf Resh Ayin Sin Tet Nun)* קְרַע שָׂטָן

‣sagevenu שַׂגְּבֵנוּ   amecha עַמְּךָ   ‣rinat רִנַּת   kabel קַבֵּל

‣nora נוֹרָא   taharenu טַהֲרֵנוּ

Accept the singing of Your Nation. Strengthen and purify us, Awesome One

---

Recite the following verse and meditate to remove the energy of death:

hatum'a הַטֻּמְאָה   ru'ach רוּחַ   ve'et וְאֶת־

‣ha'aretz הָאָרֶץ   min מִן־   a'avir אַעֲבִיר

And I will cause the unclean spirit to pass out of the land

And then immerse for the first time with mouth and eyes open.

Then immerse ten more times, one for each of the *Sefirot*:
Keter, Chochmah, Binah, Chesed, Gevurah, Tiferet, Netzach, Hod, Yesod, and *Malchut.*

There is no limit to the number of immersions one can make. The more, the better.

---

[1] According to both Kabbalah and modern physics, there are ten dimensions in our universe. The kabbalists refer to these ten dimensions as *Sefirot* (singular, *Sfirah*), meaning "emanations." The names of the dimensions from highest to lowest are *Keter, Chochmah, Binah, Chesed, Gvurah, Tiferet, Netzach, Hod, Yesod,* and *Malchut.* The *Sefirot* function like a series of curtains, each in turn gradually dimming and diminishing the intensity of Light emanating from the Creator. By the time the Light reaches the lowest level (our world of *Malchut*), it is concealed from our perception.

THE ANA BEKO'ACH

The *Ana Beko'ach* is perhaps the most powerful prayer in the entire universe. Second-century Kabbalist Rav Nachunya ben HaKana was the first sage to reveal this combination of 42 letters, which encompass the power of creation. The *Ana Beko'ach* is a unique formula, built of 42 letters written in seven sentences, that gives us the ability to transcend this physical world with all its limitations. It is known as the 42-letter Name of God. The *Ana Beko'ach* can literally remove all friction, barriers, and obstacles associated with our physical existence. It injects order into chaos, removes Satan's influence from our nature, generates financial sustenance, arouses unity with and love for others, and provides healing energy to the body and soul. We recite or scan the *Ana Beko'ach* every day, as many times as we want.

There are four elements that we connect to, using the *Ana Beko'ach*. They are:

1) **Seven Sentences** - The seven sentences correspond to the seven *Sefirot*, from *Chesed* to *Malchut*. Although there are ten *Sefirot* in total, only the lower seven exert influence in our physical world. By connecting to these seven, we seize control over this physical world.

2) **Letters of the Month** - Abraham the Patriarch revealed the astrological secrets of the Aramaic letters and of the signs of the zodiac in his kabbalistic treatise, The Book of Formation (*Sefer Yetzirah*). Each month of the year is governed by a planet, and each planet has a corresponding verse in the *Ana Beko'ach*, therefore, we also meditate upon the planet and the Aramaic letter that created both the planet and the zodiac sign of that month. (See chart on pg. 58) In doing so, we connect to the positive energy of each planet and not to its negative influence. For example, the Aramaic letter *Ayin* created the sign of Capricorn, *Tevet*. Capricorn is governed by the planet Saturn. The Aramaic letter that gave birth to Saturn is *Bet*, therefore, each day during the month of *Tevet*, we meditate upon the the letters *Ayin* and *Bet* following the recital and meditation of the first verse of the *Ana Beko'ach*.

3) **Correction of the Soul** - *Tikkun HaNefesh* - Throughout history, kabbalists have used this healing meditation twice a day, seven days a week, to regenerate and revitalize all the organs of the body. When we reach the sentence in the *Ana Beko'ach* that governs the particular month we are in, we stop and meditate on the letters of the month, and then do the *Tikkun HaNefesh*. (See pg. 59)

Using the chart as a guide, hold your right hand over the particular part of the body to which you are channeling energy. Look at the Aramaic letter combination for the specific area of the body that you are focusing on, and allow the Light to penetrate through your right hand, into that part of the body.

4) **Angels of the Day** - Angels are distinct packets of spiritual energy that act as a transportation system for our prayers. They carry our words and thoughts to the Upper Worlds. There is a line of *Ana Beko'ach* for each day of the week, and there are unique angels that govern each day. (See pg. 61-65)

❶ **Chesed**, Sunday *(Alef Bet Gimel Yud Tav Tzadik)* אבג יתץ

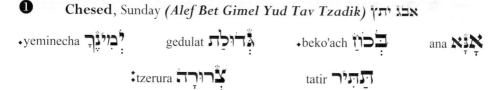

+yeminecha יְמִינֶךָ   gedulat גְּדוּלַת   +beko'ach בְּכוֹחַ   ana אָנָּא

‡tzerura צְרוּרָה   tatir תַּתִּיר

We beseech You, with the power of Your great right, undo this entanglement.

Meditation: Power of redemption. Unconditional love. Removing the negative influence of physical matter from our lives. Tapping into the Tree of Life reality. Remembering yesterday's lessons.

❷ **Gevurah**, Monday *(Kuf Resh Ayin Sin Tet Nun)* קרע שטן

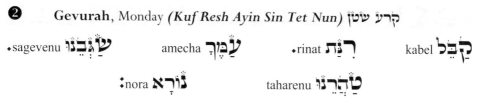

+sagevenu שַׂגְּבֵנוּ   amecha עַמְּךָ   +rinat רִנַּת   kabel קַבֵּל

‡nora נוֹרָא   taharenu טַהֲרֵנוּ

Accept the singing of Your Nation. Strengthen and purify us, Awesome One.

Meditation: Closing the gates to the Satan. Forgetting all limited and limiting thoughts. Destroying negative influences at the seed level, thus preventing bad things from happening in the first place. Overcoming our reactive nature. Transforming chaos to miracles and wonders.

❸   **Tiferet,** Tuesday *(Nun Gimel Dalet Yud Kaf Shin)* נגד יכש

•yichudecha יִחוּדְךָ   dorshei דּוֹרְשֵׁי   •gibor גִּבּוֹר   na נָא

‡shomrem שָׁמְרֵם   kevavat כְּבָבַת

Please, Mighty One, those who seek Your unity, guard them like the pupil of the eye.

Meditation: Connecting to all forms of sustenance, both physical and spiritual. Rejuvenating our body. Removing death from all aspects of life, including body, relationships, business. Gaining help to avoid speaking evil speech.

❹   **Netzach,** Wednesday *(Bet Tet Resh Tzadik Tav Gimel)* בטר צתג

•tzidkatecha צִדְקָתֶךָ   rachamei רַחֲמֵי   •taharem טַהֲרֵם   barchem בָּרְכֵם

‡gomlem גָּמְלֵם   tamid תָּמִיד

Bless them. Purify them. Your compassionate righteousness always grant them.

Meditation: Persevering. Gaining the endurance to follow through and prove victorious in our spiritual work.

❺   **Hod,** Thursday *(Chet Kuf Bet Tet Nun Ayin)* חקב טנע

•tuvcha טוּבְךָ   berov בְּרוֹב   •kadosh קָדוֹשׁ   chasin וְזְסִין

‡adatecha עֲדָתֶךָ   nahel נַהֵל

Invincible and Mighty One, with the abundance of Your goodness, govern Your congregation.

Meditation: Seeing the "big picture," thus gaining deep insight and clairvoyance into how we can connect to the Light and bring the Light to ourselves and the world.

❻ Yesod, Friday *(Yud Gimel Lamed Pei Zayin Kuf)* יגל פזק

יָחִיד yachid   גָּאֵה ge'e◦   לְעַמְּךָ le'amecha   פְּנֵה pene◦

זוֹכְרֵי zochrei   קְדֻשָּׁתֶךָ kedushatecha‡

Sole and proud One, turn to Your people, those who remember Your sanctity.

Meditation: Feeling a desire to enlighten others. Bringing spirituality to the world by spreading the wisdom of Kabbalah. Finding peace and inner tranquility.

❼ Malchut, Saturday *(Shin Kuf Vav Tzadik Yud Tav)* שקו צית

שַׁוְעָתֵנוּ shav'atenu   קַבֵּל kabel◦   וּשְׁמַע ushma   צַעֲקָתֵנוּ tza'akatenu◦

יוֹדֵעַ yode'a   תַּעֲלוּמוֹת ta'alumot‡

Accept our cry and hear our wail, You that knows all that is hidden.

Meditation: Gaining the power of renewal and restoration.

BARUCH SHEM KEVOD
Whispering this final verse brings all the Light from the Upper Worlds into our physical existence.

(Whisper) : ייזו אותיות יזוו   בָּרוּך baruch   שֵׁם shem   כְּבוֹד kevod   מַלְכוּתוֹ malchuto

וָעֶד va'ed‡   לְעוֹלָם le'olam   ריבוע ס"ג ו"י אותיות דס"ג

Blessed is the Name of Glory. His Kingdom is forever and for eternity.

LETTERS OF THE MONTH

As it mentioned above (page 54-55) of the seven planets listed, five (Saturn, Jupiter, Mars, Venus, and Mercury) control two signs each, while the sun and the moon each control one sign.

In the chart below, you can find the Aramaic letter for each month and each sign. The boxes on the right show you the corresponding verse in the *Ana Beko'ach*. Once you get to the appropriate line, pause and meditate to connect to the positive energy of that month, which is channeled to our world through the Aramaic letters.

The Month and the Letters		The Astrological Sign And the Letter		The Planet And the Letter		Ana Beko'ach meditation	
Tevet	עֵב	Capricorn	עַ	Saturn	בַ	אבג יתץ	❶
Shevat	צֵב	Aquarius	צַ	Saturn	בַ	אבג יתץ	❶
Kislev	סֵג	Sagitarius	ס	Jupiter	גַ	קרע שטן	❷
Adar	קֵג	Pisces	קַ	Jupiter	גַ	קרע שטן	❷
Nissan	דֵה	Aries	ה	Mars	דַ	נגד יכש	❸
Cheshvan	דֵנ	Scorpio	נַ	Mars	דַ	נגד יכש	❸
Av	כֵט	Leo	טַ	Sun	כ	בטר צתג	❹
Iyar	פֵו	Taurus	ו	Venus	פַ	וזקב טנע	❺
Tishrei	פֵל	Libra	לַ	Venus	פַ	וזקב טנע	❺
Sivan	רֵז	Gemini	זַ	Mercury	רַ	יגל פזק	❻
Elul	רֵי	Virgo	יַ	Mercury	רַ	יגל פזק	❻
Tammuz	וֵת	Cancer	וַ	Moon	ת	שקו צית	❼

CORRECTION OF THE SOUL - TIKKUN HANEFESH

As it mentioned above (page 54-55), throughout history, kabbalists have used this healing meditation twice a day, seven days a week, to regenerate and revitalize all the organs of the body.

Imagine you are guiding a laser beam of white Light that will penetrate each part of your body, using your right hand as a guiding tool. If there is a certain part in your body that needs extra energy, just stop and meditate on this part.

This chart represents all our body parts, each part being connected to one of the יהוה combinations – the Tetragrammaton, the *Yud Hei Vav* and *Hei*, the most powerful Name of God and the most potent tool for revealing the Lightforce in our world.

The body parts are listed and the boxes numbered, so it will be easy for you to follow the sequences, start from box no. 1 – the skull all the way to box no. 17 the feet. By meditating on these combinations of the *Yud Hei Vav* and *Hei*, you can bring this awesome Light to each part of your body.

We should also meditate for people who need healing, to send them this healing energy.

3 *Binah* Left Brain יְהֹוָה	1 *Keter* Skull יְהֹוָה	2 *Chochmah* Right Brain יְהֹוָה
5 Left Eye יהוה יהוה יהוה יהוה יהוה	9 Nose 8 יֹ יֹ הֵ הֵ וֵ וֵ הַ הַ	4 Right Eye יהוה יהוה יהוה יהוה יהוה
7 Left Ear יוד הי ואו הה		6 Right Ear יוד הי ואו הה
mouth יוד הי ואו הי (אהיה) אוזה"ע גיכ"ק דטלנ"ת זסער"ץ בומ"ף		10
12 *Gevurah* Left Arm יְהֹוָה	13 *Tiferet* Body יְהֹוָה	11 *Chesed* Right Arm יְהֹוָה
15 *Hod* Left Leg יְהֹוָה	16 *Yesod* Reproductive Organs יו הי וו הו	14 *Netzach* Right Leg יְהֹוָה
	17 *Malchut* יהואדניה	

ANGELS OF THE DAY

There are angelic forces in our lives that can help us; scanning the following prayers can activate these forces. Scan the appropriate day's prayer from right to left, making a wish while scanning. Meditate on something you need help with – overcoming fear, increasing desire, and so on – and the angelic forces will come to your aid.

יוֹם אֶ - Sunday

יֶהֹוִה

יוֹד הֵי וִיו הֵי יֵוד הֵי וָאו הֵי

אל עֹדִי יאולדִפֿהֵהִייִיאֿודֵהֹהֵיֹ

אָנָא בְּכֹחַ גְּדוּלַּת יְמִינְךָ תַּתִּיר צְרוּרָה

אַבְגִיתָץ יְהֹוָה יֶהֱוֶה

סְמַטֶּוְרֶיָה גַּזְרִיאֵל וְעָנָאֵל לְמוּאֵל (ר״ת סגול)

יוֹם בֹּ - Monday

יֵוד הֵי וָאו הֵי יוֹד הֵי וָאו הֵי יֵוד הֵי וָאו הֵא וָאו הָא

אל יֵהוֹה יאולדִפֿהֵהאאֿויאֿודֵהֹהֵאֹא

קַבֵּל רִנַּת עַמְּךָ שַׂגְּבֵנוּ טַהֲרֵנוּ נוֹרָא

קַרְעֵשְׂטָן יְהֹוֶה יֶהֱוֶה

שַׁמְעִיאֵל בִּרְכִיאֵל אַהֲנִיאֵל (ר״ת שוא)

Tuesday - יום גֹּ

יוֹד הֹא וֹאוֹ הֹא יוֹד הֹהֹ וֹו הֹהֹ

אל אדֹנֹי יאוֹלדֹפֹההֹהֹהֹויֹווֹדֹהֹהֹהֹ

נֹא גֹבוֹר דוֹרשֹי יוֹזוֹדֹך כֹבבֹת שֹמרם

נֹגְדִיכֶשֹ יֱהֹוֶה יהֹוֹה

וֹנִיאֹל לֹהֹדִיאֹל מוֹזֹנִיאֹל (ר״ת וֹזלם)

Wednesday - יום דֹ

יוֹד הֹא וֹאוֹ הֹא יוֹד הֹהֹ וֹו הֹהֹ

אל אדֹנֹי יאוֹלדֹפֹההֹהֹהֹויֹווֹדֹהֹהֹהֹ

ברכם טֹהרם רוֹזֹמֹי צֹדקֹתֹך תֹמֹידֹ גֹמלם

בַּטְֹרְצַֹתֹג יֱהֹוֶה יהֹוֹה

וֹזֹקֹיאֹל רהֹטִיאֹל קֹדֹשִׁיאֹל (ר״ת וֹזרקֹ)

Thursday - יום הֵ

יוּד הֵי וָאו הֵי יוּד הֵי וָאו הֵי יוּד הֵא וָאו הֵא

אל יהוה יאולדפההאאויאוודההאא

וזסין קָדוֹש בְּרוֹב טוּבְך נהל עֲדָתֶך

וַקְבֶטנַע יְהֶוֹה יְהֹוָה

שְׁמוֹעָאל רְעֶמִיאֵל קְנִיאֵל

(ר"ת שׂרק – הֹקְבוֹץ מֹלאכיו בר"ת שׂוֹרק)

Friday - יום וו

יוּד הֵי וָיו הֵי יוּד הֵי וָאו הֵי

אל עֲדִי יאולדפההיייאואודההיי

יוֹזִיד גָאה לעַמְך פְּנה זוכרי קְדוֹשָׁתֶך

יָגְלפָזָק יְהֶוֹה יֻהֹוָוהֹו

שׂובוֹעֲשׂיוִיאוֹלוֹ רופוֹאוֹלוֹ קוּדוֹשׂיוִיאוֹלוֹ (ר"ת שׂרק)

As it metioned above, There are angelic forces in our lives that can help us.

On Shabbat, as we ascend through our prayers to the Upper Worlds we can connect to the Angels of Friday night (See hereby pg. 64), Saturday morning (See pg. 65) and Saturday afternoon (See pg. 65).

Angels of Friday night

יוּד הֵי וָאו הֵי

שׁוֹעָתֵנוּ קַבֵּל וּשְׁמַע צַעֲקָתֵנוּ יוֹדֵעַ תַּעֲלוּמוֹת

שַׁקּוּצִית יֱהֹוֶה יְהֹוָה יֱהֹוֶה

שְׁמְעִיאֵל בְּרַכִיאֵל אֲהַנִיאֵל (ר"ת שׁוא)

סַמְטוּרְיָה גּוּרִיאֵל וְעָנָאֵל לְמוּאֵל (ר"ת סֶגּוֹל)

צוּרִיאֵל רְזִיאֵל יוֹפִיאֵל (ר"ת צירי)

Angels of *Shabbat* (Saturday) Morning

יוֹד הֵי וִיו הֵי יוֹד הֵי יוֹד הֵי וִיו הֵי

שַׁוְעָתֵנוּ קַבֵּל וּשְׁמַע צַעֲקָתֵנוּ יוֹדֵעַ תַּעֲלוּמוֹת

עַקְוְצִית יְהֹוֶה יְהֹוֶה יְהֹוֶה

שִׁמְעִיאֵל בִּרְכִיאֵל אַהֲנִיאֵל (ר"ת שׁוא)

קַדְמִיאֵל מַלְכִיאֵל צוּרִיאֵל (ר"ת קמ"ץ)

Angels of *Shabbat* (Saturday) Afternoon

יוֹד הֵא וָאו הֵא יוֹד הֵא וָאו הֵא

שַׁוְעָתֵנוּ קַבֵּל וּשְׁמַע צַעֲקָתֵנוּ יוֹדֵעַ תַּעֲלוּמוֹת

עַקְוְצִית יְהֹוֶה יְהֹוֶה יְהֹוֶה

שִׁמְעִיאֵל בִּרְכִיאֵל אַהֲנִיאֵל (ר"ת שׁוא)

פַּדְאֵל תַּלְמִיאֵל (תּוּמִיאֵל) וְזַסְדִּיאֵל (ר"ת פתוז)

THE SHEMA

There are few *Shema* connections during the day.

One of them is said in the morning, and another is said before going to bed (See pg. 88).

The *Shema* is one of the most powerful tools to draw the energy of healing to our lives. The true power of the *Shema* is unleashed when we meditate upon others who need healing energy while reciting it.

Before we actually start the *Shema*, we must think about the concept of loving our neighbors as we love ourselves.

The first verse of the *Shema* (*Shema Yisrael...*) channels the energy of *Zeir Anpin*, or the Upper Worlds.

The second verse (*Baruch shem...*) refers to our world, the World of *Malchut*.

There are a total of 248 words in this prayer, and these 248 words transmit healing energy to the 248 parts of the human body and its soul.

The first paragraph of the *Shema* is built of 42 words, connecting us to the 42-Letter Name of God in the *Ana Beko'ach*.

The second paragraph is composed of 72 words that connect us to The 72 Names of God.

The third paragraph contains 50 words that link us to The 50 Gates of *Binah*, which helps us rise above the 50 Gates of Negativity.

The final paragraph of the *Shema* has 72 words, which also connects us to The 72 Names of God, but through a different letter combination than that which is used in the second paragraph.

We cover our eyes while saying the first two verses: *Shema Yisrael* and *Baruch Shem Kevod.* , and reciting the rest with deep meditation, saying it with the intonations.

Adonai יְהֹוָה‎(אֲדֹנָי־אהדונהי) ע׳ רבתי יִשְׂרָאֵל Yisrael שְׁמַע shema

אֱלֹהֵינוּ Elohenu יל׳ ד׳ רבתי echd אֶחָד‎ | Adonai יְהֹוָה‎(אֲדֹנָי־אהדונהי) אֱחָד‎ | echad ; אהבה, דאגה׃

(Whisper :) יחו אותיות בָּרוּךְ baruch שֵׁם shem כָּבוֹד kevod מַלְכוּתוֹ malchuto,

וָעֶד va'ed׃ ריבוע דס״ג י׳ אותיות דס״ג le'olam לְעוֹלָם

Yud, Chochmah, head — 42 words corresponding to the Holy 42-Letter Name of God.

א

אֵת et (ה׳ אהבת על מ״ע לקיים כיון ;‎ ב״פ אין סוף, ב״פ רו, ב״פ אור,‎) ve'ahavta וְאָהַבְתָּ

ת

יְהֹוָה‎(אֲדֹנָי־אהדונהי) Adonai מושיוו בן דוד ע״ה כהת, ס״ת ; יל׳ Elohecha אֱלֹהֶיךָ

ק ר צ

נַפְשֶׁךָ nafshecha לכב, ב״ן uvchol וּבְכָל levavcha לְבָבְךָ ב״ן, לכב bechol בְּכָל

ט ש ע

הַדְּבָרִים hadevarim vehayu וְהָיוּ me'odecha מְאֹדֶךָ׃ לכב ,ב״ן uvchol וּבְכָל

י ד ג ג

metzavecha מְצַוְּךָ anochi אָנֹכִי asher אֲשֶׁר ha'ele הָאֵלֶּה

ב ש כ

לְבָבֶךָ levavecha׃ עַל al (pause here) אֶל יהוה, ז׳, מזבוו, נגד, ע״ה hayom הַיּוֹם

Hear Israel, the Lord our God. The Lord is One.
Blessed is the glorious Name, His Kingdom is forever and for eternity.
And you shall love the Lord, your God, with all your heart and with all your soul and
with all that you possess. Let those words that I command you today be upon your heart.

ת   צ   ר   ט

מ"ב   bam בָּם   vedibarta וְדִבַּרְתָּ   levanecha לְבָנֶיךָ   veshinantam וְשִׁנַּנְתָּם

ק   וו   ג

uvlechtecha וּבְלֶכְתְּךָ   ב"פ ראה   bevetecha בְּבֵיתֶךָ   beshivtecha בְּשִׁבְתְּךָ

ו   ט   ב

uvkumecha וּבְקוּמֶךָ:   uvshochbecha וּבְשָׁכְבְּךָ   ב"פ יב"ק, ס"ג קס"א vaderech בַדֶּרֶךְ

ל   ג   י   ע

yadecha יָדֶךָ   al עַל־   le'ot לְאוֹת   ukshartam וּקְשַׁרְתָּם

ק   ו   פ

ben בֵּין   letotafot לְטֹטָפֹת   vehayu וְהָיוּ

י   ק   ש

al עַל־   uchtavtam וּכְתַבְתָּם   מ"ה: רִבּוּעַ ; קס"א ע"ה enecha עֵינֶיךָ

ת   י   צ

uvish'arecha וּבִשְׁעָרֶיךָ:   betecha בֵּיתֶךָ ב"פ ראה   נית (זו מות) mezuzot מְזוּזוֹת

And you shall teach them to your children and you shall speak of them while you sit in your home and while you walk on your way and when you lie down and when you rise. You shall bind them as a sign upon your hand and they shall be as frontlets between your eyes. And you shall write them upon the doorposts of your house and your gates.

Hei, Binah, arms and body — 72 words corresponding to the 72 Names of God.

יכי

והו

דאהיה ע״ה דמילוי ודמילוי ודמילוי דמילוי, דפשוט אותיות מ״א יוה״ך ; יהוה **אִם**־ im יהוה vehaya **וְהָיָה**

לכלה   מוהשע   עלם   סיט

mitzvotai **מִצְוֹתַי**   el **אֶל**־   tishme'u **תִּשְׁמְעוּ**   shamo'a **שָׁמֹעַ**

אלד   הזי   כהת   אכא

etchem **אֶתְכֶם**   metzave **מְצַוֶּה**   anochi **אָנֹכִי**   asher **אֲשֶׁר**

ההע   לאו

דאגה אוזד, le'ahava **לְאַהֲבָה** (pause here) אל יהוה ז״ן, מזבוח, נגד, ע״ה hayom **הַיּוֹם**

הרי   מבה   יזל

ילה   Elohechem **אֱלֹהֵיכֶם**   Adonai **יְהֹוֶה**אהדונהיאהדונהי   et **אֶת**־

לאו   הקם

לכב ב״ן, bechol **בְּכָל**־   ul'ovdo **וּלְעָבְדוֹ** (enunciate the letter *Ayin* in the word "*ul'ovdo*")

פהל   לוו   כלי

nafshechem **נַפְשְׁכֶם**   לכב   ז״ן, uvchol **וּבְכָל**־   levavchem **לְבַבְכֶם**

And it shall come to be that if you shall listen to My commandments that I am commanding you with today to love the Lord, your God, and to serve Him with all your heart and with all your soul.

נלך	יויי	מולה	וזהו
venatati וְנָתַתִּי	metar מְטַר	artzechem אַרְצְכֶם	be'ito בְּעִתּוֹ

נתה	האא	ירת	שׂאה
yore יוֹרֶה	umalkosh וּמַלְקוֹשׁ	ve'asafta וְאָסַפְתָּ	deganecha דְּגָנֶךָ

ריי	אום	לכב	ועור
vetiroshcha וְתִירֹשְׁךָ	veyitz'harecha וְיִצְהָרֶךָ	venatati וְנָתַתִּי	esev עֵשֶׂב ע"ב שומות

יווו	להוו	כוך	מנגד
besadcha בְּשָׂדְךָ	livhemtecha לִבְהֶמְתֶּךָ	ve'achalta וְאָכַלְתָּ	vesavata וְשָׂבָעְתָּ

אני	וזעם	רהע	יין	ההה
hishamru הִשָּׁמְרוּ	lachem לָכֶם	pen פֶּן	yifte יִפְתֶּה	levavchem לְבַבְכֶם

מיכ	וול	ילה	סאל
vesartem וְסַרְתֶּם	va'avadetem וַעֲבַדְתֶּם	elohim אֱלֹהִים	acherim אֲחֵרִים

משה (העומד) נגד הקליפות)	עלע	ערי
vehishtachavitem וְהִשְׁתַּחֲוִיתֶם	lahem לָהֶם

מיה	והו	דני	הויע
vechara וְחָרָה	af אַף (pause here)	Adonai יהוה	bachem בָּכֶם

Then I shall send rain upon your land in its proper time, both early rain and late rain. You shall then gather your grain and your wine and your oil. And I shall give grass in your field for your cattle. And you shall eat and you shall be satiated. Be careful lest your heart be seduced and you may turn away and serve alien deities and prostrate yourself before them. And the wrath of the Lord shall be upon you

עמם וְעָצַ֣ר ve'atzar   נגא אֶת־ et   נית הַשָּׁמַ֗יִם hashamayim   מובה י"פ טל, י"פ כוזו וְלֹא־ velo

פוי יִהְיֶ֣ה yihye   נמם יְיָ מָטָ֔ר matar   ייל וְהָ֣אֲדָמָ֔ה veha'adama   מצר לֹ֥א lo תִתֵּ֖ן titen

ומב אֶת־ et   יהה יְבוּלָ֑הּ yevula   עלו וַאֲבַדְתֶּ֣ם va'avadetem   דמב מְהֵרָ֗ה mehera   עלם מֵעַל֙ me'al

מנק הָאָ֨רֶץ ha'aretz   אלהים הַטֹּבָ֜ה hatova   איע אֲשֶׁ֣ר asher

ראה יְיָ Adonai   יבמ נֹתֵ֣ן noten   היי לָכֶ֑ם lachem **Vav, Zeir Anpin**

מום וְשַׂמְתֶּם֙ vesamtem **stomach** — 50 words corresponding to the 50 Gates of *Binah*

א אֶת־ et   ה דְּבָרַ֣י devarai   ' אֵ֔לֶּה ele   ה עַל־ al

א לְבַבְכֶ֖ם levavchem   ה וְעַֽל־ ve'al   ' נַפְשְׁכֶ֑ם nafshechem

and He shall stop the Heavens and there shall be no more rain and the earth shall not give forth its crop. And you shall quickly perish from the good land that the Lord has given you. And you shall place those words of Mine upon your heart and upon your soul

וּקְשַׁרְתָּם ukshartem — אֹתָם otam — לְאוֹת le'ot — ר"ת לאו — עַל־ al — יֶדְכֶם yedchem

וְהָיוּ vehayu — לְטֹטָפֹת letotafot — בֵּין ben — עֵינֵיכֶם enechem — ריבוע מ"ה:

וְלִמַּדְתֶּם velimadetem — אֹתָם otam — אֶת־ et — בְּנֵיכֶם benechem

לְדַבֵּר ledaber — בָּם bam — ראה — עם בן מ"ב — בְּשִׁבְתְּךָ beshivtecha

בְּבֵיתֶךָ bevetecha — ב"פ ראה — וּבְלֶכְתְּךָ uvlechtecha — בַדֶּרֶךְ vaderech — ב"פ יב"ק, ס"ג קס"א

וּבְשָׁכְבְּךָ uvshochbecha — וּבְקוּמֶךָ uvkumecha: — וּכְתַבְתָּם uchtavtam — עַל־ al

מְזוּזֹות mezuzot — בֵּיתֶךָ betecha — ב"פ ראה — וּבִשְׁעָרֶיךָ uvish'arecha:

*and you shall bind them as a sign upon your hands and they shall be as frontlets between your eyes.
And you shall teach them to your children and speak of them while you sit at home
and while you walk on your way and when you lie down and when you rise.
You shall write them upon the doorposts of your house and upon your gates.*

ה   י   ה

ייל'   ר"ת   yemechem **לְמֵיכֶם**   yirbu **יִרְבּוּ**   lema'an **לְמַעַן**

ה   י   ה   א

ha'adama **הָאֲדָמָה**   al **עַל**   venechem **בְּנֵיכֶם**   vimei **וִימֵי**

אהיה   אהיה

יכוין לשבועת המבול   nishba **נִשְׁבַּע** (enunciate the letter *Ayin* in the word "*nishba*")   asher **אֲשֶׁר**

אהיה   אהיה   אהיה

latet **לָתֵת**   la'avotechem **לַאֲבֹתֵיכֶם**   Adonai **יְהֹוָה**   אדניאהדונהי

אהיה   אהיה   אהיה

כוזו   י"פ   טל'   י"פ   hashamayim **הַשָּׁמַיִם**   kimei **כִּימֵי**   lahem **לָהֶם**

אהיה   אהיה   אהיה

ע"ה:׃   ההין   אלהים   ha'aretz **הָאָרֶץ**   al **עַל**

This is so that your days shall be numerous and so shall the days of your children upon the Earth that the Lord had sworn to your fathers to give them as the days of the Heavens upon the Earth.

Hei, *Malchut*, **legs and reproductive organs,**

72 words corresponding to the 72 Names of God in direct order (according to the Ramchal).

עאם	סבט	ייי	ווו
Moshe מֹשֶׁה	el אֶל־	Adonai יְהֹוָֽהאהדונהי	vayomer וַיֹּ֥אמֶר

מהש"ע, ע"ב ברי**ב**וע וקס"א, אל שדי, ד"פ אלהים ע"ה

אנא	ליה	מבה	
el אֶל־	daber ראה דַּבֵּ֞ר	lemor לֵאמֹֽר	

המוע	להו	אנד	כמת
ve'asu וְעָשׂ֨וּ	alehem אֲלֵהֶ֜ם	ve'amarta וְאָמַרְתָּ֣	benei בְּנֵ֤י
		Yisrael יִשְׂרָאֵל֙	

לוו	הבם	היי	מרה	יצל
vigdehem בִגְדֵיהֶ֖ם	kanfei כַּנְפֵ֥י	al עַל־	tzitzit צִיצִ֛ת	lahem לָהֶ֥ם

נמם	פהל	ליו	כבי
tzitzit צִיצִ֥ת	al עַל־	venatnu וְנָֽתְנ֛וּ	ledorotam לְדֹרֹתָ֑ם

וההו	מנה	יהו
techelet תְּכֵֽלֶת׃	petil פְּתִ֥יל	hakanaf הַכָּנָ֖ף

ע"ה קנ"א, אדני אלהים י"פ ב"ן

And the Lord spoke to Moses and said: Speak to the Children of Israel and say to them that they should make for themselves Tzitzit, on the corners of their garments, throughout all their generations. And they must place upon the Tzitzit, of each corner, a blue strand.

וְהָיָ֨ה vehaya ; יהוה ; יהוה   לָכֶ֜ם lachem   לְצִיצִת֒ letzitzit   וּרְאִיתֶ֣ם ur'item   אֹת֗וֹ oto

וּזְכַרְתֶּם֙ uzchartem   אֶת־ et   כָּל־ kol   מִצְוֺ֣ת mitzvot   יְהֹוָ֔ה Adonai

וַעֲשִׂיתֶ֖ם va'asitem   אֹתָ֑ם otam   וְלֹֽא־ velo   תָת֜וּרוּ taturu   אַחֲרֵ֣י acharei

לְבַבְכֶם֙ levavchem   וְאַחֲרֵ֣י ve'acharei   עֵֽינֵיכֶ֔ם enechem

אֲשֶׁר־ asher   אַתֶּ֥ם atem   זֹנִ֖ים zonim   אַחֲרֵיהֶֽם׃ acharehem   לְמַ֣עַן lema'an

תִּזְכְּר֔וּ tizkeru   וַעֲשִׂיתֶ֖ם va'asitem   אֶת־ et   כָּל־ kol   מִצְוֺתָ֑י mitzvotai

וִהְיִיתֶ֥ם vihyitem   קְדֹשִׁ֖ים kedoshim   לֵאלֹהֵיכֶֽם׃ lelohechem

And this shall be to you as a Tzitzit: you shall see it and remember the commandments of the Lord and fulfill them. And you shall not stray after your hearts and your eyes, after which you adulterate. This is so that you shall remember to fulfill all My commandments and thereby be holy before your God.

הבו ⟶ asher אֲשֶׁר ‏ילה Elohechem אֱלֹהֵיכֶם Adonai יְהֹוָﬡדﬠﬡﬡﬣﬧﬧﬠﬣ אני ani אֲנִﬤ ⟵ פאי

עלו ⟶ Mitzrayim מִצְרַיִם me'eretz מֵאֶרֶץ etchem אֶתְכֶם hotzeti הוֹצֵאתִי ⟵ מזר
מצר ‏ואה ‏והב

מכק ⟶ lelohim לֵאלֹהִים lachem לָכֶם lihyot לִהְיוֹת ⟵ מזו
ילה ; אדני אהיה ‏דהב

רלה ⟶ Elohechem אֱלֹהֵיכֶם Adonai יְהֹוָﬡדﬠﬡﬡﬣﬧﬧﬠﬣ אני ani אֲנִﬤ ⟵ אלﬠ
ילהﬤﬤ ‏וזהו

אֱמֶת emet אהיה פעמים אהיה, ז"פ ס"ג◆

You should repeat the last three words as with these three words the 248 words of *Shema* are completed.

הלﬤ ⟶ Elohechem אֱלֹהֵיכֶם Adonai יְהֹוָﬡדﬠﬡﬡﬣﬧﬧﬠﬣ ⟵ ﬤﬤﬦ
ﬤﬤﬣﬤﬤ

מוהם ⟶ **אֱמֶת** emet אהיה פעמים אהיה, ז"פ ס"ג◆

I am the Lord, your God, Who brought you out of the land of Egypt to be your God.
I, the Lord, your God, Is true. The Lord, your God, is true!

MEDITATION FOR SUSTENANCE

Everything comes from the Light. As long as we always remain aware of this fact when we receive good fortune in our lives, the fulfillment it generates will stay with us forever. On the other hand, when we prosper but believe that we are the architects of our own success, we draw our prosperity from the Satan. If this is our consciousness, eventually we will lose whatever we have gained or we will "pay" for it in some other area of our life, which we can see from the many people in this world who are successful, for example, in business only to be burdened with various tragedies in other areas of their lives, for example, their marriages or children.

Everything comes with a price. The price might be extracted in ten years' or ten minutes' time, but eventually, we *will* pay if we do not fully appreciate that our good fortune comes solely from the Light. The money and success that we are destined to receive is going to come to us anyway. Our free will lets us choose whether it comes from the Light through our appreciation or from the Satan with our ego telling us that we are responsible for our success. We have two ways to protect ourselves:

1) Recognize that all good fortune comes from the Light.

2) Use a percentage of our earnings to help others — the concept of tithing (explanation and meditaion – pg. 81).

hu הוּא	berich בְּרִיךְ	kudsha קוּדְשָׁא	yichud יִוזוּד	leshem לְשֵׁם
ur'chimu וּרְוזִימוּ (יאההיויהה),	bid'chilu בַּדְוזִילוּ	(יאההינהי)	ush'chintei וּשְׁכִינְתֵיהּ	
shem שֵׁם	leyachada לְיַוזַדָא (איההיויהה),	ud'chilu וּדְוזִילוּ	ur'chimu וּרְוזִימוּ	
(יהוה) shelim שְׁלִים	beyichuda בְּיִוזוּדָא	kei קֵי	bevav בְּואו"ו	kei קֵי	yud יו"ד
hareni הֲרֵינִי	Yisrael יִשְׂרָאֵל,	יל	kol כָּל	beshem בְּשֵׁם
holech הוֹלֵךְ	oh אוֹ	zu זוּ	bimlacha בִּמְלָאכָה	matchil מַתְוזִיל
ze זֶה.	umatan וּמַתָּן	masa מַשָּׂא	oh אוֹ	ze זֶה	le'esek לְעֵסֶק

For the sake of unification between The Holy Blessed One and His Shechinah, with fear and love, and with love and fear, in order to unify the Name Yud-Kei and Vav-Kei in perfect unity, and in the name of all Israel, I am hereby start this activity, or this business, or this negotiation.

יְהִי yehi רָצוֹן ratzon מהשׁע ע״ה, ע״ב בר־יבוע וקס״א ע״ה, אל שדי ע״ה

מִלְּפָנֶיךָ milfanecha ס״ג מ״ה ב״ן יְהֹוָואהדונהי Adonai אֱלֹהֵינוּ Elohenu ילה

וֵאלֹהֵי velohei לכב ; מילוי ע״ב, דמב ; ילה אֲבוֹתֵינוּ avotenu שֶׁתִּשְׁלַח shetishlach

הַצְלָחָה hatzlacha בְּכָל vechol ב״ן, לכב מַעֲשֵׂה ma'ase יָדַי yadai

וּתְפַרְנְסֵנִי utfarneseni בְּכָבוֹד bechavod בוכי שֶׁלֹּא shelo אֶצְטָרֵךְ etztarech

לִידֵי lidei מַתְּנַת matnot בָּשָׂר basar וָדָם vadam וְלֹא velo לִידֵי lidei

הַלְוָאָתָם halva'atam כִּי ki אִם im יוהר, מ״א אותיות אהיה בפשוטו ומילואו ומילוי דמילואו ע״ה

לְיָדְךָ leyadcha וְיִהְיֶה vesheyihye יי כִּי li פָּנַאי penai פוי, אל אדני

בִּירָאָה beyir'a כִּי ki אַתָּה Ata אֵל El ייא״י טוֹב tov והי לְכֹל lakol יה אדני

וּמֵכִין umechin מָזוֹן mazon לְכָל lechol יה אדני בְּרִיּוֹתֶיךָ beriyotecha

דִכְתִיב: dichtiv נֹתֵן noten אבג יתץ, ועד לֶחֶם lechem ג׳ הויות לֶכֹם lechol יה אדני

בָּשָׂר basar ר״ת = יב״ק, אלהים יהוה, אהיה אדני יהוה כִּי ki לְעוֹלָם le'olam

רִיבוע ס״ג ו׳ אותיות דס״ג הויות, מזלא (להמשיך הארה ממזלא עילאה) ; ר״ת = נגה: חַסְדּוֹ chasdo ג׳ הויות

May it be pleasing before You, the Lord, my God and God of my forefathers, that You send success in all my handwork, and You will sustain me with dignity, so I will not need people's largesse and not their loan, but only Your hand. So I will be leisure to worship you with awe. Because You are good God for everyone and prepare food to all of Yours creation. As it says: "He gives nourishment to all flesh, for his kindness endures forever."

At this point, we open our hands and hold the palm up while we meditate on these combinations.

פּוֹתֵחַ pote'ach **אֶת** et **יָדֶךָ** yadecha

ר״ת פַּאי וס״ת וזתך (עם ג' אותיות = דִיקָרְנוֹסָא) ובאתב״ש הוא סאל, אמן, יאהדונהי ;
ועוד יכוין עם וזתך בעילוב יהוה כזה: יְוֹזְהְתוֹכֶךְ המסוגל לפרנסה)

וּמַשְׂבִּיעַ umasbi'a

וזתך (עם ג' אותיות = דִיקָרְנוֹסָא) ובאתב״ש הוא סאל, פאי, אמן, יאהדונהי ;
ועוד יכוין עם וזתך בעילוב יהוה כזה: יְוֹזְהְתוֹכֶךְ המסוגל לפרנסה)

לְכָל lechol **וָ"וֹ** chai וז׳׳ = אהיה אהיה יהוה, בינה ע׳׳ה, וז׳׳ים

רָצוֹן ratzon מהע ע׳׳ה, ע׳׳ב ברבוע וקס׳׳א ע׳׳ה, אל עדי ע׳׳ה; ר׳׳ת רוזל שהיא המלכות הצריכה לעהפע׃

וְתַמְצִיא vetamtzi **לִי** li **עַל** al **יָדֵי** yedei **מְלָאכָה** melacha **זוּ** zu

אוֹ oh **עֵסֶק** esek **זֶה** ze, **אוֹ** oh **מַשָּׂא** masa **וּמַתָּן** umatan **זֶה** ze **כְּדֵי** kedei

שֶׁאוּכַל she'uchal **לְפַרְנֵס** lefarnes **בְּנֵי** benei **בֵּיתִי** beti, **כְּלֶחֶם** lechem ג׳ היוות

לֶאֱכוֹל le'echol **וּבֶגֶד** uveged **לִלְבּוֹשׁ** lilbosh **וּשְׁמַע** ushma **תְּפִלָּתִי** tefilati **כִּי** ki

אַתָּה Ata **שׁוֹמֵעַ** shome'a **תְּפִלַּת** tefilat **עַמְּךָ** amecha **יִשְׂרָאֵל** Yisrael

בְּרַחֲמִים berachamim מצפצ, אלהים דיודין, י׳׳פ ייי **בָּרוּךְ** baruch **אַתָּה** Ata

שׁוֹמֵעַ shome'a **תְּפִלָּה** tefila א׳׳ת ב׳׳ש אוכצ, ב׳׳ן אדני וניקודה ע׳׳ה יוד הי ו הה׃

"Open Your Hands and give fulfillment to every living creature's desire."
And You will deliver me by this activity, or this business, or this negotiation, so I can sustain my family and my household with bread to eat and clothing to wear, and hear my prayer, for You hear the prayer of your people Yisrael with compassion. Bless are You, who hears prayers.

MEDITATION FOR GIVING TZEDAKAH (CHARITY)

Meditate that your action of *Tzedakah* connects you to *Yesod* of Ima of *Zeir Anpin* that is called "*Gabai Tzedakah*" – the *Tzedakah* collector, who collects all the illuminations and gives it to the poor, which is the world of *Malchut*.

Also meditate on the word *Tzedakah* צְדָקָה to bring *Yesod* (male) and *Malchut* (female) together, as follows:

The letter *Tzadik* צ:

The shape of the letter *Tzadik* is as the letter *Nun* (female) and the letter *Yud* (male) back-to-back.
Meditate to connect *Zeir* and *Nukva* face-to-face.

The letter *Dalet* ד:

The name of the letter *Dalet* comes from the word *Dalut* in Hebrew which means poverty. Also, the shape of the letter *Dalet* (*Malchut*) is like the letter *Hei* (corrected *Malchut*) but empty inside.
Meditate to fulfil the poor (*Malchut*) and connect it with the letter *Yud* (*Yesod*) to form the letter *Hei*.

The letter *Kof* ק:

The shape of the letter *Kof* is similar to the letter *Hei* (corrected *Malchut*) but with long leg. The long leg actually feeds the negative side.
Meditate to cut the leg of the letter *Kof*, and make it similar to the letter *Hei* so as not to feed the *Kelipa*.

The letter *Hei* ה: To connect all above (the letters *Tzadik, Dalet* and *Kof*) to the corrected *Malchut* (the letter *Hei*).

Also meditate, using the Tetragrammaton Name [יהוה *Yud, Hei, Vav* and *Hei*], to remove the gap between the Upper world and our world, as follows:

The letter *Yud* י – represents the money that is being giving to *Tzedakah*.

The letter *Hei* ה – represents the hand (palm) of the giver that holds the *Tzedakah*.

The letter *Vav* ו – represents the arm that hands over the money to the receiver (the *Gabai Tzedakah*).

The last letter *Hei* ה – represents the hand (palm) of the receiver.

MEDITATION FOR GIVING MA'ASER (TITHING)

There are two kinds of wealth: spiritual and physical. The concept of tithing--giving away 10% of our earnings--is designed to remove Satan's influence from our lives. If Satan remains attached to our financial sustenance, eventually this influence will wither away our good fortune. Tithing does not diminish our well-being. On the contrary, it protects our sustenance and brings greater prosperity and joy to every area of our lives.

Scanning the excerpt from the Zohar, *Mikketz* below enhances our connection to Joseph the Righteous, who is the channel of *Zeir Anpin* and is our funnel to receive Light from the Upper Worlds.

106. וְיוֹסֵף veYosef הוּא hu הַשַׁלִּיט hashalit עַל al הָאָרֶץ ha'aretz וְגוֹ' vego, ר' Rabbi יִסָּא Yesa פָּתַח petach וְעַתָּה ve'ata יָרוּם yarum רֹאשִׁי roshi עַל al וַיֹּאמַר va'amar וְאֶזְבְּחָה ve'ezbecha בְּאָהֳלוֹ be'aholo זִבְחֵי zivchei סְבִיבוֹתַי sevivotai אוֹיְבַי oyvai תְּרוּעָה teru'a אֲשִׁירָה ashira וַאֲזַמְּרָה va'azamra לַי"י laHashem. ת"ח ta-chaze, כַּד kad קָבָ"ה Kudsha-Berich-Hu אִתְרְעֵי itre'ei בֵּיה beh בְּבַר bevar נָשׁ nash, זָקִיף zakef לֵיה leh עַל al כָּל kol בְּנֵי benei עָלְמָא alma, וְעָבֵיד ve'aved לֵיה leh רֵישָׁא resha דְּכֹלָא dechola, וְכֻלְהוּ vechul'hu שַׂנְאוֹי san'oi אִתְכַּפְיָין itkafyan תְּחוֹתוֹי techotoi.

107. דָּוִד David מַלְכָּא Malka, שַׂנְאוּ san'u לֵיה leh אֲחוֹי achoi, דְּוָוֹ dacho לֵיה leh עַל al כָּל kol מִנַּיְיהוּ minai'hu, קָבָ"ה Kudsha-Berich-Hu אָרֵים arem לֵיה leh עַל al כָּל kol בְּנֵי benei עָלְמָא alma, אָתָא ata וְזַמּוֹי chamoi עָרַק arak בְּמִקָּמֵיה mikamei, קָבָ"ה Kudsha-Berich-Hu אָרֵים arem לֵיה leh עַל al כָּל kol מַלְכוּתֵיה malchuteh, וְכֻלְהוּ vechul'hu הֲוֹו havo כָּרְעִין kar'in וְסָגְדִין vesagdin קָמֵיה kameh. וְיוֹסֵף veYosef דְּוָחוּ dachu לֵיה leh אֲחוֹי achoi, לְבָתַר levatar כֻּלְהוּ kul'hu סָגִידוּ usgidu קָמֵיה kameh, כָּרְעוּ kar'u הה"ד hada-hu-dichtiv וַיָּבֹאוּ vayavo'u אֲחֵי achei יוֹסֵף Yosef וַיִּשְׁתַּחֲוֹו vayish'tachavu לֹו lo אַפַּיִם apayim אַרְצָה artza.

108. ד"א, davar-acher, וְעַתָּה ve'ata יָרוּם yarum רָאשִׁי roshi, מַאי mai וְעַתָּה ve'ata, כְּמוֹ kemo וְאַתָּה ve'ata. ר' Rabbi יְהוּדָה Yehuda אָמַר amar, הָא ha אִתְּמַר itmar, עֵת et דְּאִיהוּ de'ihu דַּרְגָּא darga עִלָּאָה ila'a, וּמַאן uman אִיהוּ ihu הַהוּא hahu עֵת et. דָּא da ה"א hei, וְאִקְרֵי ve'ikrei עַתָּה ata, וְעַתָּה ve'ata: דָּא da אִיהוּ ihu וּבֵי uvei דִּינֵיהּ dinei.

109. יָרוּם yarum רָאשִׁי roshi, לַאֲרָמָא la'arama לֵהּ la בִּיקָרָא bikara וּמַלְכוּתָא umalchuta. עַל al אוֹיְבַי oyvai סְבִיבוֹתַי sevivotai, אִלֵּין ilen שְׁאָר she'ar מַלְכֵי malchei אַרְעָא ara'a. וְאָזְבְּחָה ve'ezbecha בְּאָהֳלוֹ be'aholo, דָּא da יְרוּשָׁלַיִם Yerushalayim, בְּאָהֳלוֹ be'aholo דָּא da אֹהֶל ohel מוֹעֵד moed. זִבְחֵי zivchei תְרוּעָה teru'a, לְמִשְׁמַע lemishma כָּל kol עָלְמָא alma. אָשִׁירָה ashira וַאֲזַמְּרָה va'azamra, מֵהַהוּא mehahu סִטְרָא sitra דְּתְרוּעָה ditru'a הִיא hee, דְּהָא deha מִתַּמָּן mitaman, מֵהַהוּא mehahu סִטְרָא sitra דְּתְרוּעָה ditru'a, הִיא hee אַתְיָא atya שִׁירָה shira וְתוּשְׁבְּחָתָּא vetushbachta.

110. ד"א, davar-acher, וְעַתָּה ve'ata יָרוּם yarum רָאשִׁי roshi, דָּא da כְּנֶסֶת Keneset יִשְׂרָאֵל Yisrael. עַל al אוֹיְבַי oyvai סְבִיבוֹתַי sevivotai, דָּא da עֵשָׂו esav וְכָל vechol אַפַּרְכִין afarchin דִּילֵיהּ dileh. וְאֶזְבְּחָה ve'ezbecha בְּאָהֳלוֹ be'aholo, אִלֵּין ilen יִשְׂרָאֵל Yisrael. זִבְחֵי zivchei תְרוּעָה teru'a, דִּכְתִיב dichtiv זִבְחֵי zivchei אֱלֹקִים Elokim רוּוַח ru'ach נִשְׁבְּרָה nishbara, בְּגִין begin לְאַעֲבָרָא le'a'avara דִּינָא dina בְּעָלְמָא me'alma. אָשִׁירָה ashira וַאֲזַמְּרָה va'azamra, לְאוֹדָאָה le'oda'a וּלְשַׁבְּוֹתָא ul'shabecha לְקָב"ה leKudsha-Berich-Hu בְּלָא bela פְּסִיקוּ pesiku לְעוֹלָם le'olam.

111. ד"א, davar-acher, וְעַתָּה ve'ata יָרוּם yarum רָאשִׁי roshi, בְּכֹלָּא bechola יֵצֶר yetzer טוֹב tov עַל al יֵצֶר yetzer רָע ra, דִּכְתִיב dichtiv עַל al אוֹיְבַי oyvai סְבִיבוֹתַי sevivotai,

דָּא da יֵצֶר yetzer הָרַע hara, דְּאִיהוּ de'ihu סוֹחֲרָנֵיהּ sacharaneh דְּבַר devar נָשׁ nash,

וְאִיהוּ ve'ihu שַׂנְאֵיהּ san'eh בְּכֹלָּא bechola. וְאֶזְבְּחָה ve'ezbecha בְּאָהֳלוֹ ve'aholo,

זִבְחֵי zivchei תְּרוּעָה teru'a דָּא da אוֹרַיְיתָא orayta, דְּאִתְיְהִיבַת de'ityehivat

מִסִּטְרָא misitra דְּאֶסָא de'esa, כִּדְכְתִיב kedichtiv בִּימִינוֹ mimino

אֵשׁ esh דָּת dat לָמוֹ lamo, דְּהָא deha בְּגִין begin אוֹרַיְיתָא orayta,

יְרוּם yarum רֵישֵׁיהּ reisheh, וְאִתְבָּרוּ ve'itavru כָּל kol שַׂנְאוֹי sano'i

קֳדָמוֹי kodamoi, כִּדְכְתִיב kedichtiv תַּכְרִיעַ tachri'a קָמַי kamai תַּחְתָּי tachtai.

.112   ד"א davar-acher, וְעַתָּה ve'ata יְרוּם yarum רֹאשִׁי roshi,

לְאִתְכְּלָלָא le'itkelala בַּאֲבָהָן ba'avahan דְּהָא deha דָּוִד David מַלְכָּא Malka,

אִית it לֵיהּ leh לְאִתְדַּבְּקָא le'itdabaka בַּאֲבָהָן ba'avahan, וּכְדֵין uchden

יִתְרוֹמֵם yitromem וְסָלֵיק vesalek לְעֵילָא le'ela, וְאִיהוּ ve'ihu בְּחַד bechad

קְשׁוּרָא kishura בְּהוֹ beho. עַל al אוֹיְבֵי oyvai סְבִיבוֹתַי sevivotai, אִלֵּין ilen אִינוּן inun

דְּבִסְטַר devistar שְׂמָאלָא semala, כֻּלְּהוּ kulhu מָארֵי marei דִּינִין dinin,

דְּמִתְכַּוְּנִין demitkavnin לְחַבָּלָא lechabala, וּכְדֵין uchden שִׁמְשָׁא shimsha

אִתְחַבַּר itchabar בְּסִיהֲרָא besihara, וְהָוֵי vahavei כֹּלָּא kola וַד chad.

.113   ת"ו ta-chaze, כְּתִיב ketiv וְיוֹסֵף veYosef הוּא hu הַשַּׁלִּיט hashalit עַל al

הָאָרֶץ ha'aretz, דָּא da שִׁמְשָׁא shimsha דְּשַׁלִּיט deshalit בְּסִיהֲרָא besihara,

וְנָהִיר venaher לָהּ la, וְזָן vezan לָהּ la. הוּא hu הַמַּשְׁבִּיר hamashbir לְכָל lechol עַם am

הָאָרֶץ ha'aretz, דְּהָא deha הַהוּא hahu נְהַר nahar דְּנָגֵיד denaged וְנָפֵיק venafek,

מִנֵּיהּ mineh אִתְּזָנוּ itzanu כֻּלְּהוּ kulhu, וּמִתַּמָּן umitaman פָּרְחִין parchin

נִשְׁמָתִין nishmatin לְכֹלָּא lechola, וּבְגִין uvgin דָּא da כֻּלְּהוּ kulhu סַגְדִּין sagdin

לְגַבֵּיהּ legabeh דְּהַהוּא dehahu אֲתָר atar, דְּהָא deha לֵית let לָךְ lach מִלָּה mila

בְּעָלְמָא be'alma, דְּלָא dela תֲּלֵי talei בְּמַזָּלָא bemazala וְאוֹקְמוּהָ ve'okmuha.

MEDITAION FOR HEALING

The Aramaic letters *Mem* בּו, *Hei* ה, *Shin* עי release the force of healing. We should close our eyes and visualize these three letters emitting rays of Light, bathing our entire body in a flood of white Light. We should also send this energy to others in need of healing. We can meditate upon the person's name or visualize the *Mem Hei Shin* radiating Light over their body. These letters, rearranged, also spell out the name of Moshe מהשע = משה.

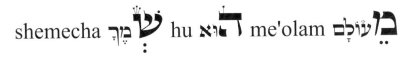

shemecha בִּמְךָ שֶׁ שֶׁ hu הוּא me'olam מֵעוֹלָם

Has always been Your Name

This special paragraph from the Zohar, Pinchas will help us enhance the healing energy.

436. וּבְחִבּוּרָא קַדְמָאָה, פָּתַח רַעְיָא מְהֵימְנָא וְאָמַר, וַוי לוֹן לִבְנֵי נָשָׁא, דְּאִינוּן אֲטִימִין לִבָּא, סְתִימִין עַיְנִין, דְּלָא יַדְעִין אֵבָרִים דְּגוּפַיְהוּ עַל מָה אִינוּן מִתְתַּקְנִין, דְּהָא קָנֵ״ה תְּלַת וְלֵין כְּלִילָן בֵּיה, וְזַד הֶבֶל, דְּאִיהוּ לַהַב אֵשׁ, דְּנָפִיק מִן לִבָּא וְאִתְפְּלַג לוֹ' הֲבָלִים, דְּאָמַר קֹהֶלֶת. תִּנְיָינָא, אֲוִיר דְּעָאל לְגַבֵּיה מִלְּבַר. תְּלִיתָאָה, מַיִם דְּכַנְפֵּי רֵיאָה, דְּאִינוּן דְּבוּקִים בְּקָנֶה. וּמִתְּלַת אִלֵּין אִתְעֲבִיד קוֹל, מַיִם וְרוּחַ וְאֵשׁ, וּמִתְפְּלַג כָּל וַזַד לוֹ', וְאִינוּן ז' לְהָבִים, ז' אֲוִירוֹת, ז' נְוָזלִים.

436. *And in the first section, the Faithful Shepherd started by saying, "Woe to those people whose hearts are closed and whose eyes are unseeing, who do not know the parts of their own body, according to what they are arranged." For the trachea is composed of three forces: a) Vapor (Heb. hevel, hei bet lamed), which is a flame (Heb. lahav, lamed hei bet), a flaming fire that issues from the heart and which is divided into seven vapors or vanities as mentioned by Kohelet (Ecclesiastes); b) Air, which enters it from outside; c) Water of the wings of the lung, which are attached to the trachea. And from these three, that is from water, wind, and fire, is voice made, and each one is subdivided into seven, and they are seven flames, seven airs, and seven brooks.*

BLESSING FOR SHABBAT CANDLES

We light the Shabbat candles to draw the spiritual Light into our personal lives. Every physical action in our world initiates a corresponding reaction in the Upper Worlds. By lighting the physical candles of Shabbat with the consciousness and intent to connect to the energy of Shabbat in the Upper Worlds, we arouse and draw spiritual Light into our physical world.

A secret of the candles can be found in their numerical value of 250. When we light two candles their numerical is 250 x 2 = 500. A man has 248 bone segments and joints, whereas a woman has 252. Together, 248 + 252 = 500, the same value as two candles. This signifies the power of one soul, the unity between a man and a woman.

All souls in the Upper World are comprised of both male and female in equal halves. When a particular soul comes to this world of Malchut, it splits into two: male and female separately. If two people are soul mates, but they find themselves living on opposite sides of the globe, the woman's action of lighting two candles helps bring these two halves of one soul closer together. By virtue of this simple act of lighting the candles, they can find each other and reunite as one soul.

When a woman lights the Shabbat candles, she is also helping to correct the sin of Eve, which was a Desire to Receive for the Self Alone. The action of lighting the candles becomes an act of sharing. Because the husband and children are closest to the woman, they receive the benefit of this action.

On a Shabbat that does not coincide with a holiday, we say the following blessing. We light the candles first, then encircle the candles with our hands three times to draw the light towards our face. We cover our eyes and recite the blessing.

בָּרוּךְ baruch אַתָּה Ata יְהֹוָֹהאֲדֹנָיאֲהַדְוָנָהי Adonai

אֱלֹהֵינוּ Elohenu יְלֹה מֶלֶךְ melech הָעוֹלָם ha'olam אֲשֶׁר asher

קִדְּשָׁנוּ kideshanu בְּמִצְוֹתָיו bemitzvotav וְצִוָּנוּ vetzivanu לְהַדְלִיק lehadlik

נֵר ner יהוה אהיה יהוה אלהים יהוה אדני שֶׁל shel שַׁבָּת Shabbat:

Blessed are You, Lord, our God, King of the world,
Who has sanctified us with His commandments and obliged us with lighting the candles of Shabbat.

BLESSING FOR HOLIDAY CANDLES

(Should be followed by the blessing of *Shehecheyanu* on pg. 87)

If a holiday falls on Shabbat, we should recite two blessings over the candles: one for Shabbat and one for the holiday. These special blessings are said only on holidays, and they connect us to the extra energy revealed on that holiday. We light the candles first, then encircle the candles with our hands three times to draw the light towards our face. We cover our eyes and recite the blessing.

בָּרוּךְ baruch אַתָּה Ata יְהֹוָֹהאֲדֹנָיאֲהַדְוָנָהי Adonai

אֱלֹהֵינוּ Elohenu יְלֹה מֶלֶךְ melech הָעוֹלָם ha'olam

אֲשֶׁר asher קִדְּשָׁנוּ kideshanu בְּמִצְוֹתָיו bemitzvotav וְצִוָּנוּ vetzivanu

לְהַדְלִיק lehadlik נֵר ner יהוה אהיה יהוה אלהים יהוה אדני שֶׁל shel

(if the holiday falls on Shabbat add : שַׁבָּת Shabbat (וְ ve) יוֹם yom טוֹב tov:

Blessed are You, Lord, our God, King of the world, Who has sanctified us
with His commandments and obliged us with lighting the candles of (Shabbat and) the holiday.

BLESSING FOR YOM KIPPUR CANDLES

(Should be followed by the blessing of *Shehecheyanu* hereby on pg. 87)

For Yom Kippur, there is a special blessing. We light the candles first, then encircle the candles with our hands three times to draw the light towards our face. We cover our eyes and recite the blessing.

בָּרוּך baruch אַתָּה Ata יְהֹוָ/אדני/יאהדונהי Adonai

אֱלֹהֵינוּ Elohenu יהוה מֶלֶךְ melech הָעוֹלָם ha'olam

אֲשֶׁר asher קִדְּשָׁנוּ kideshanu בְּמִצְוֹתָיו bemitzvotav וְצִוָּנוּ vetzivanu

לְהַדְלִיק lehadlik נֵר ner יהוה אהיה יהוה אלהים יהוה אדני שֶׁל shel

(וְ ve) שַׁבָּת Shabbat : if Yom Kippur falls on Shabbat add)

יוֹם yom הַכִּפּוּרִים hakipurim:

Blessed are You, Lord, our God, King of the world, Who has sanctified us
with His commandments and obliged us with lighting the candles of (Shabbat and) the Day of Atonement.

BLESSING OF SHEHECHEYANU

בָּרוּך baruch אַתָּה Ata יְהֹוָ/אדני/יאהדונהי Adonai אֱלֹהֵינוּ Elohenu יהוה

מֶלֶךְ melech הָעוֹלָם ha'olam שֶׁהֶחֱיָנוּ shehecheyanu

וְקִיְּמָנוּ vekiyemanu וְהִגִּיעָנוּ vehigi'anu לַזְּמַן lazeman הַזֶּה haze:

Blessed are You, Lord, our God, King of the world,
who has kept us alive, sustained us, and brought us to this time.

The Shema Reading at Bedtime

After enduring the rigors and adversity associated with the day, the soul is drained. Each night, our soul ascends to the Upper Realms for recharging and rejuvenation. Even if we remain awake, a part of soul departs when the sun has set and the stars have begun to appear in the heavens, which is why we feel more tired as the night unfolds. The more negative we are, the more drained we feel when this part of our soul leaves our body. Each night, there is an actual force that induces us to sleep to allow our soul to vacate our body. We recite the Bedtime *Shema* to attach an umbilical chord to our soul so that is will return and fill the space it has left behind.

LeShem Yichud

Before we begin the *Shema*, we recite *LeShem Yichud*. *LeShem Yichud* acts like a spark plug, activating the next series of prayers and actions.

hu **הוּא**   berich **בְּרִיךְ**   kudsha **קֻדְשָׁא**   yichud **יִחוּד**   leshem **לְשֵׁם**

(יאהדוּיהה) ur'chimu **וּרְחִימוּ** bid'chilu **בִּדְחִילוּ** (יאהדוֹנהי) ush'chintei **וּשְׁכִינְתֵיהּ**

shem **שֵׁם**   leyachda **לְיַחֲדָא**   (איההויהה) ud'chilu **וּדְחִילוּ** ur'chimu **וּרְחִימוּ**

(יהוה) shelim **שְׁלִים** beyichuda **בְּיִחוּדָא** kei **קֵי** bevav **בְּוא"ו** kei **קֵי** yud **יוּ"ד**

For the sake of unification between the Holy Blessed One and His Shechinah, with fear and love and with love and fear, in order to unify the Name Yud, Kei and Vav, Kei in perfect unity,

בְּשֵׁם beshem כָּל kol יְלֵי ,יִשְׂרָאֵל Yisrael הֲרֵינִי hareni מְקַבֵּל mekabel

עָלַי alai אֱלֹהוּתוֹ Elahuto יִתְבָּרֵךְ yitbarach וְאַהֲבָתוֹ ve'ahavato

וְיִרְאָתוֹ veyir'ato וַהֲרֵינִי vehareni יָרֵא yare מִמֶּנּוּ mimenu בְּגִין begin

דְּאִיהוּ de'ihu רַב rav וְשַׁלִּיט veshalit עַל al כּוּלָּא kula, וְכוּלָּא vechula

קַמֵּיהּ kamei כֹּלָּא kela, וַהֲרֵינִי vehareni מַמְלִיכוֹ mamlicho עַל al כָּל kol

מֵרַמַ"ח meramach וְגִיד vagid וְגִיד vegid וְאֵבֶר ve'ever אֵבֶר ever; עמ' יְלֵי

אֲבָרִים evarim אברהם, וז"פ אל, רי"ו ול"ב נתיבות הוחכמה, רמ"וז (אברים), עסמ"ב וט"ז אותיות פעוטות

וְשַׁסַּ"ה ruchi רוּוֵזִי, וְנַפְשִׁי venafshi גּוּפִי gufi שֶׁל shel עַל al גִּידִים gidim veshasa

וְנִשְׁמָתִי venishmati מַלְכוּת malchut גְּמוּרָה gemura וּשְׁלֵמָה ushlema,

וַהֲרֵינִי vaharani עֶבֶד eved לְהַשֵּׁם leHashem יִתְבָּרֵךְ yitbarach, וְהוּא vehu

בְּרַחֲמָיו berachamav בוכי יְזַכֵּנִי yezakeni לְעָבְדוֹ le'ovdo בְּלֵבָב belevav

שָׁלֵם shalem וְנֶפֶשׁ venefesh וַחֲפֵצָה chafetza אָמֵן amen יאהדונהי

כֵּן ken יְהִי yehi רָצוֹן ratzon מהע ע"ה, ע"ב ברבוע וקס"א ע"ה, אל שדי ע"ה:

and in the name of all Israel, I hereby accept upon myself His divinity, blessed be He, and the love of Him and the fear of Him. And I hereby fear Him for being great, He Who reigns over everything. Before Him, everything is insignificant. I hereby accept His Sovereignty over each and every organ and each and every sinew of the 248 (a woman says 252) organs and 365 sinews of my body, with lower spirit, my Neshamah and soul as a complete and perfect sovereignty. And I hereby declare myself a servant of the Lord, blessed be He. May He, in His mercy, allow me the privilege of serving Him wholeheartedly and with a willing spirit. Amen, so may it be His will.

RIBONO SHEL OLAM

Before we recite this prayer, we should reflect on our day and search for any negativity that we may have caused others, or that others may have caused us. If a person goes to sleep harboring any ill feeling toward another person, this feeling will prevent both souls from elevating to the Upper Worlds during the night. In this prayer, we ask for forgiveness from those people to whom we caused pain. We acknowledge that this forgiveness applies to everything that occurred, whether intentional or accidental, through words or through physical activity, in this lifetime or in past lifetimes. The concept of forgiving others has nothing to do with the person we are forgiving. Spiritually, forgiveness is about letting go of our anger and resentments. Kabbalistically, the people who hurt us in life are merely messengers. We should never blame the messenger. All our prior actions, positive or negative, are subject to a boomerang effect and will eventually return to us through the deeds of others.

mochel **מוֹחֵל**   hareni **הֲרֵינִי**   olam **עוֹלָם**   shel **שֶׁל**   Ribono **רִבּוֹנוֹ**

shehich'is **שֶׁהִכְעִיס**   mi **מִי**   lechol **לְכָל**   vesole'ach **וְסוֹלֵחַ**

kenegdi **כְּנֶגְדִּי** ◆   shechata **שֶׁחָטָא**   oh **אוֹ**   oti **אוֹתִי**   vehiknit **וְהִקְנִיט**

bichvodi **בִּכְבוֹדִי**   ben **בֵּין**   bemamoni **בְּמָמוֹנִי**   ben **בֵּין**   begufi **בְּגוּפִי**   ben **בֵּין**

be'ones **בְּאוֹנֶס**   ben **בֵּין**   li **לִי** ◆   asher **אֲשֶׁר**   bechol **בְּכָל**   ben **בֵּין**

beratzon **בְּרָצוֹן**   ben **בֵּין**

bemezid **בְּמֵזִיד**   ben **בֵּין**   beshogeg **בְּשׁוֹגֵג**   ben **בֵּין**

bema'ase **בְּמַעֲשֶׂה** ◆   ben **בֵּין**   bedibur **בְּדִבּוּר**   ben **בֵּין**

Master of the World, I hereby forgive and pardon anyone who has angered or has irritated me or has sinned against me, whether against my body, my money, my honor, or anything else that is mine; whether by force or willingly, whether by mistake or wantonly, whether through speech or action;

ben בֵּין   begilgul בְּגִלְגּוּל   ze זֶה   ben בֵּין   begilgul בְּגִלְגּוּל   acher אַחֵר

lechol לְכָל   bar בַּר   Yisrael יִשְׂרָאֵל   velo וְלֹא   ye'anesh יֵעָנֵשׁ

shum שׁוּם   adam אָדָם   besibati בְּסִבָּתִי   yehi יְהִי   ratzon רָצוֹן

Adonai יְהֹוָה   milfanecha מִלְפָנֶיךָ

Elohai אֱלֹהַי   velohei וֵאלֹהֵי

avotai אֲבוֹתַי   shelo שֶׁלֹּא   echeta אֶחֱטָא   od עוֹד

uma וּמַה   shechatati שֶׁחָטָאתִי   lefanecha לְפָנֶיךָ

mechok מְחוֹק   berachamecha בְּרַחֲמֶיךָ   harabim הָרַבִּים   aval אֲבָל

lo לֹא   al עַל   yedei יְדֵי   yisurin יִסּוּרִין   vechola'im וָחֳלָאִים   ra'im רָעִים

מ"ב אותיות בפסוק

yih'yu יִהְיוּ   leratzon לְרָצוֹן

imrei אִמְרֵי   fi פִי   vehegyon וְהֶגְיוֹן   libi לִבִּי

lefanecha לְפָנֶיךָ   Adonai יְהֹוָה   tzuri צוּרִי   vego'ali וְגֹאֲלִי

whether in this incarnation or any past lifetime, or from any of the Children of Israel, and may no one be punished on my behalf. May it be Your will, Lord, my God and God of my fathers, that I will not sin again. And any sin that I have already committed before You, erase with Your bountiful compassion, but not by means of suffering or evil illnesses. "May the utterances of my mouth and the thoughts of my heart be favorable before You, Lord, my Rock and my Redeemer."

HAMAPIL

This blessing ensures that our soul safely departs during sleep and returns to our body upon awakening. It is the lifeline between the body and the soul.

> If you go to sleep **before midnight**, you say the entire blessing (from *"baruch Ata"* to *"bichvodo"*).
> If you go to sleep **after midnight**, you skip the words *"Adonai Eloheinu melech ha'olam"*
> at the beginning of the blessing, and the words *"Ata Adonai"* at the end of the blessing.

ילה אֱלֹהֵינוּ Elohenu יְהֹוָה/אדני/אהדונהי Adonai אַתָּה Ata בָּרוּךְ baruch

וְחֶבְלֵי chevlei הַמַּפִּיל hamapil הָעוֹלָם ha'olam מֶלֶךְ melech

עַל al וּתְנוּמָה utnuma דמ"ה רבוע enai עֵינַי al עַל shena שֵׁנָה

עֲפַעַפַּי afapai וּמֵאִיר ume'ir לְאִישׁוֹן le'ishon בַּת bat עַיִן ayin רבוע דמ"ה

יְהִי yehi רָצוֹן ratzon מוהש ע"ה ע"ב בריבוע וקס"א ע"ה, אל עדי ע"ה

אֱלֹהַי Elohai יְהֹוָה/אדני/אהדונהי Adonai ב"ן מ"ה ס"ג milfanecha מִלְפָנֶיךָ

אֲבוֹתַי avotai ; ילה דמב, דע"ב מילוי ; לכב דע"ב מילוי ; velohei וֵאלֹהֵי ילה ; דמב דע"ב, מילוי

וְתַעֲמִידֵנִי veta'amideni לְשָׁלוֹם leshalom שֶׁתַּשְׁכִּיבֵנִי shetashkiveni

וּלְשָׁלוֹם ulshalom◆ טוֹבִים tovim אהיה יהוה, בינה ע"ה בינה אהיה אהיה lechayim לְחַיִּים

Blessed are You, Lord, Our God, King of the world, Who causes the bonds of sleep to fall upon my eyes and slumber upon my lids, and Who brings the light of sight to the pupil of my eye. May it be pleasing before You, Lord, my God and God of my fathers, that You may lay me down in peace and make me rise to a good life and to peace,

וְתֵן veten | חֶלְקִי chelki | בְּתוֹרָתֶךְ betoratecha | וְתַרְגִּילֵנִי vetargileni

לִדְבַר lidvar | מִצְוָה mitzva | רָאה | וְאַל ve'al | תַּרְגִּילֵנִי targileni

לִדְבַר lidvar | עֲבֵרָה avera | רָאה | וְאַל ve'al | תְּבִיאֵנִי tevi'eni | לִידֵי lidei

וְטֵא chet | וְלֹא velo | לִידֵי lidei | נִסָּיוֹן nisayon | וְלֹא velo | לִידֵי lidei

בִּזָּיוֹן vizayon | וְיִשְׁלוֹט veyishlot | בִּי bi | יֵצֶר yetzer | הַטּוֹב hatov | והו

וְאַל ve'al | יִשְׁלוֹט yishlot | בִּי bi | יֵצֶר yetzer | הָרָע hara

וְתַצִּילֵנִי vetatzileni | מִיֵּצֶר miyetzer | הָרָע hara | וּמֵחֳלָאִים umechola'im

רָעִים ra'im | וְאַל ve'al | יְבַהֲלוּנִי yavhiluni | וְחֲלוֹמוֹת chalomot

רָעִים ra'im | וְהִרְהוּרִים vehirhurim | רָעִים ra'im | וּתְהֵא utehe

מִטָּתִי mitati | שְׁלֵמָה shelema | לְפָנֶיךָ lefanecha | ס״ג מ״ה ב״ן | וְהָאֵר vehaer

עֵינַי enai | דמ״ה | ריבוע | פֶּן pen | אִישַׁן ishan | הַמָּוֶת hamavet

בָּרוּךְ baruch | אַתָּה Ata | יְהוָֹה אדני אהיה אהדונהי Adonai | הַמֵּאִיר hame'ir

לְעוֹלָם la'olam | ריבוע דס״ג וי׳ אותיות דס״ג | כֻּלּוֹ kulo | בִּכְבוֹדוֹ bichvodo׃

and that You may give me my portion in Your Torah and accustom me to observe the commandments and not accustom me to transgressions. Do not lead me to sins, to trials, or to shame. Let the good inclination govern me and do not allow the evil inclination to control me. And save me from the evil inclination and from evil illnesses. Do not let bad dreams or evil thoughts frighten me. Let my bed be complete before You. Enlighten my eyes lest I sleep a sleep of death. Blessed are You, Lord, Who illuminates the whole world with His glory.

THE SHEMA (at this point we say the Shema – See pages 66-76)

YA'ALZU

Every negative act we perform produces negative angels that surround us each and every day. These negative entities are often the unseen cause of all those things that go wrong in our lives. These verses help remove the negative angels and their destructive influence.

Chasidim וַחֲסִידִים ג״פ אם אותיות דפשוטM, דמילוי ודמילוי דמילוי הג״פ אהיה ya'lezu יַעְלְזוּ

:mishkevotam מִשְׁכְּבוֹתָם al עַל־ yeranenu יְרַנְּנוּ בוכי bechavod בְּכָבוֹד

bigronam בִּגְרוֹנָם (ה״ג) (מילוי) ייא״י El אֵל romemot רוֹמְמוֹת

ר״ת קנ״א ב״ן, יהוה אלהים אדני, מילוי קס״א וס״ג, מ״ה ברבוע וע״ב ע״ה

:beyadam בְּיָדָם pifiyot פִּיפִיּוֹת רי״ו vecherev וְחֶרֶב

The pious shall exult in glory and sing joyously upon their beds.
High praises of God in their throats and a double edged sword in their hands.

HINE MITATO SHELISHLOMO

The kabbalists teach us that sleep is 1/60th of death. It is important to ask ourselves: "Did I do enough spiritual change in my life today? Am I happy if this should be my last day?"

The next verse contains 20 words; they are recited three times (20 x 3 = 60) to correspond to the 1/60th of death that occurs when we sleep.

Meditate that by going to sleep you elevate your soul, as you depart now from the world.

ר"ת מהש, שֶׁלִּשְׁלֹמֹה sheliShlomo מִטָּתו mitato הִנֵּה hine

ע"ב ברבוע וקס"א, אל שדי, ד"פ אלהים ע"ה גִּבֹּרִים giborim שִׁשִּׁים shishim

כֻּלָּם kulam יִשְׂרָאֵל: Yisrael מִגִּבֹּרֵי migiborei לָהּ la סָבִיב saviv

אִישׁ ish מִלְחָמָה milchama מְלֻמְּדֵי melumedei חֶרֶב cherev אֲחֻזֵי achuzei

בַּלֵּילוֹת: balelot מִפַּחַד mipachad יְרֵכוֹ yerecho עַל־ al רי"ו charbo וְחַרְבּוֹ

Behold the bed of Solomon: sixty mighty men surround it from among the mighty ones of Israel. They are all armed with swords and trained in battle, each with his sword ready by his side through fear of the nights. [

BLESSING OF THE KOHANIM

There are 60 words in this section, which help our soul to be elevated without the negative aspect of death.

יְהֹוָאדֹנָיאהדונהי Adonai יְבָרֶכְךָ yevarechecha יְבָרֶכְךָ (Right – *Chesed*)

ר"ת = יהוה ; וס"ת = מ"ה: וְיִשְׁמְרֶךָ veyishmerecha וְיִשְׁמְרֶךָ

פָּנָיו panav | Adonai יְהֹוָאדֹנָיאהדונהי כף ויי זין ויי ya'er יָאֵר (Left - *Gevurah*)

אֵלֶיךָ elecha מנד ; יהה אותיות בפסוק vichuneka וִיחֻנֶּךָּ elecha אֵלֶיךָ

elecha אֵלֶיךָ panav פָּנָיו | Adonai יְהֹוָאדֹנָיאהדונהי yisa יִשָּׂא (Central – *Tiferet*)

האא תיבות בפסוק: shalom שָׁלוֹם lecha לְךָ veyasem וְיָשֵׂם

(Right) *May the Lord bless you and protect you.*
(Left) *May the Lord shine His Countenance upon you and be gracious to you.*
(Central) *May the Lord turn His Face towards you and give you peace.*

Yoshev Beseter Elyon

There are 60 words in this section, which help our soul to be elevated without the negative aspect of death.

יֹשֵׁב yoshev   בְּסֵתֶר beseter   ב"פ מצר   עֶלְיוֹן elyon   בְּצֵל betzel   שַׁדַּי Shadai

יִתְלוֹנָן: yitlonan   אֹמַר omar   לַיהוָֹה(אדני-אהדונהי) ladonai   מַחְסִי machsi

וּמְצוּדָתִי umtzudati   אֱלֹהַי Elohai   מילוי דע"ב, דמב ; ילה ; ר"ת אום, מובה, יזל

אֶבְטַח evtach   סיט   בּוֹ: bo   כִּי ki   הוּא hu   יַצִּילְךָ yatzilcha

מִפַּח mipach   ר"ת   מויה   יָקוּשׁ yakush   מִדֶּבֶר midever   הַוּוֹת: havot

בְּאֶבְרָתוֹ be'evrato   יָסֶךְ yasech   לָךְ lach   וְתַחַת־ vetachat   כְּנָפָיו kenafav

תֶּחְסֶה techse   צִנָּה tzina   וְסֹחֵרָה vesochera   אֲמִתּוֹ: amito   לֹא־ lo   תִירָא tira

מִפַּחַד mipachad   לָיְלָה layla   מילה   מֵחֵץ mechetz   יָעוּף ya'uf   יוֹמָם: yomam

One who finds refuge in the supreme One and dwells in the shade of Shaddai, I say of Lord: He is my Refuge and my Fortress, my God in Whom I put my trust. He shall rescue you from the snare of the trap and from destructive pestilence. He shall cover you with His Pinion and you shall find refuge under His Wings. His Truth is a shield and armor. You shall not fear the terrors of the night, the arrow that flies by day.

מִדֶּבֶר midever	בָּאֹפֶל ba'ofel	יַהֲלֹךְ yahaloch	מִקֶּטֶב miketev
יָשׁוּד yashud	צָהֳרָיִם tzahorayim:	יִפֹּל yipol	מִצִּדְּךָ mitzidcha
אֶלֶף elef המספר אלף = אלף למד עיין דלת יוד ע"ה	וּרְבָבָה urvava	בְּימִינֶךָ miminecha	
אֵלֶיךָ elecha	לֹא lo	יִגָּשׁ yigash:	רַק rak	בְּעֵינֶיךָ be'enecha ע"ה קס"א ; ריבוע דמ"ה	תִרְאֶה tir'e:
תַבִּיט tabit	וְשִׁלֻּמַת veshilumat	רְשָׁעִים resha'im			
כִּי ki	אַתָּה Ata	יְהֹוָה Adonai אדני יאהדונהי	מַחְסִי machsi ◆		

the pestilence that moves in the darkness, or the destruction that strikes at noon.
A thousand will fall at your side and ten thousand at your right, yet they will not approach you. You shall
merely look with your eyes and see the retribution of the wicked, because You, the Lord, are my Refuge.

VIDUI – AWARENESS AND ACKNOWLEDGMENT

The next two sections ("*ashamnu…*" and "*yehi ratzon…*" on pg. 98-99) are to be said only on weekdays,
not on *Shabbat*, holidays or *Rosh Chodesh*, also not on Tzadikim death anniversaries.

All our wrongful actions leave a residue on our body. Reciting and connecting with *Vidui* and *Yehi Ratzon* cleanses away all these negative remnants, working like the fast on *Yom Kippur*.

While reciting the Vidui, you should strike your chest with the right hand and meditate to shake the *Chasadim* (mercy) and the *Gevurot* (judgment) so they can grow up for the sake of the *Zivug* (unification).

Even if you know that you didn't commit one of the below-mentioned negative actions, you should still say the *Vidui*. Because we are all act as guarantors to each other. The *Vidui* is said in plural because the *Vidui* is about other lifetimes and other people who are connected to your soul's root.

אָנָּא ana ב״ן יְהֹוָ‎ה/אדני‎ה/אהדונהי Adonai אֱלֹהֵינוּ Elohenu יכה

וֵאלֹהֵי velohei לכב ; מילוי ע״ב, דמב ; יכה אֲבוֹתֵינוּ avotenu. תָּבֹא tavo

לְפָנֶיךָ lefanecha ס״ג מ״ה ב״ן תְּפִלָּתֵנוּ tefilatenu וְאַל ve'al תִּתְעַלַּם tit'alam

מַלְכֵּנוּ malkenu מִתְּחִנָּתֵנוּ.mit'chinatenu שֶׁאֵין she'en אָנוּ anachnu

עַזֵּי azei אלהים ע״ה, אהיה אדני ע״ה פָּנִים fanim וּקְשֵׁי ukshei עֹרֶף oref

לוֹמַר lomar ס״ג מ״ה ב״ן לְפָנֶיךָ lefanecha מ״ה ב״ן יְהֹוָ‎ה/אדני‎ה/אהדונהי Adonai

אֱלֹהֵינוּ Elohenu יכה וֵאלֹהֵי velohei לכב ; מילוי ע״ב, דמב ; יכה

אֲבוֹתֵינוּ avotenu צַדִּיקִים tzadikim אֲנוּ anachnu וְלֹא־ velo

וְחָטָאנוּ.chatanu אֲבָל aval חָטָאנוּ.chatanu וְחָטָאנוּ.chatanu עָוִינוּ.avinu פָּשַׁעְנוּ.pashanu

אֲנוּ anachnu וַאֲבוֹתֵינוּ va'avotenu וְאַנְשֵׁי ve'anshei בֵיתֵנוּ vetenu ב״פ ראה:

אָשַׁמְנוּ.ashamnu בָּגַדְנוּ.bagadnu גָּזַלְנוּ.gazalnu דִּבַּרְנוּ dibarnu דּוֹפִי dofi

וְלָשׁוֹן velashon הָרַע hara הֶעֱוִינוּ.he'evinu וְהִרְשַׁעְנוּ.vehirshanu זַדְנוּ.zadnu

וְזַמַּסְנוּ chamasnu טָפַלְנוּ tafalnu שֶׁקֶר sheker וּמִרְמָה umirma.יָעַצְנוּ ya'atznu

עֵצוֹת etzot רָעוֹת ra'ot כִּזַּבְנוּ.kizavnu כָּעַסְנוּ.ka'asnu לַצְנוּ.latznu

מָרַדְנוּ.maradnu מָרִינוּ marinu דְּבָרֶיךָ.devarecha נִאַצְנוּ.ni'atznu

We beseech You, Lord, our God and the God of our fathers. May our prayer come before You and may Our King not ignore our plea. For we are not arrogant and stiff necked to say before You Lord, our God and the God of our fathers that we are righteous and we did not sin. For we have sinned, we have committed iniquity, we have transgressed, we and our fathers and the people of our household. **א** *We are guilty,* **ב** *we betrayed,* **ג** *we stole,* **ד** *we spoke gossip and evil speech,* **ה** *we caused iniquity,* **ו** *we convicted,* **ז** *we were wanton,* **ח** *we robbed,* **ט** *we accused falsely and deceitfully,* **י** *we gave bad advice,* **כ** *we lied,* **ך** *we have anger,* **ל** *we mocked,* **מ** *we revolted,* **ם** *we rebelled Your commandments,* **נ** *we gave contempt,*

נְאָפְנוּ ni'afnu • סָרַרְנוּ sararnu • עָוִינוּ avinu • פָּשַׁעְנוּ pashanu • פָּגַמְנוּ pagamnu •

צָרַרְנוּ tzararnu • צִעַרְנוּ tzi'arnu • אָב av וָאֵם va'em • קִשִּׁינוּ kishinu • עֹרֶף oref •

רָשַׁעְנוּ rashanu • שִׁחַתְנוּ shichatnu • תִּעַבְנוּ ti'avnu • תָּעִינוּ ta'inu • וְתִעְתַּעְנוּ veti'atanu

וְסַרְנוּ vesarnu • מִמִּצְוֹתֶיךָ mimitzvotecha • וּמִמִּשְׁפָּטֶיךָ umimishpatecha

הַטּוֹבִים hatovim • וְלֹא velo • שָׁוָה shava • לָנוּ lanu • אֱלֹהִים, elohim, • אֶהְיֶה • אֲדֹנָי.

וְאַתָּה veAta • צַדִּיק tzadik • עַל al • כָּל kol • הַבָּא haba • עָלֵינוּ alenu • כִּי ki

אֱמֶת emet • עָשִׂיתָ asita • וַאֲנַחְנוּ va'anachnu • הִרְשָׁעְנוּ hirsha'nu

:Meditate to ensure that your negative actions are part of the past and are not part of your present anymore

we committed adultery, ס *we have been perverted,* ע *we caused wickedness,* פ *we transgressed,* צ *we damaged,* צ *we have oppressed,* ק *we gave sorrow to our mother and father,* ק *we were stubborn,* ר *we have been wicked,* ש *we have corrupted,* ת *we committed abominations, we have gone astray from Your commandments and good laws, and it has not benefited us. For You are righteous regarding whatever has befallen us, for You have acted truthfully and we caused wickedness.*

יְהִי רָצוֹן מהש"ע ע"ה, ע"ב ברבוע וקס"א וקס"א ע"ה, אל שדי ע"ה, מִלְּפָנֶיךָ ס"ג מ"ה ב"ן יְהֹוָאֱדֹנָ[יْ]אֱלֹהִֽים אֱלֹהֵֽינוּ ילה וֵאלֹהֵי אֲבוֹתֵֽינוּ ילה שֶׁאָם וְחָטָֽאתִי וּמֵאם ; מילוי דע"ב, דמב ; יֶלֶה אֲבוֹתֵֽינוּ ס"ג מ"ה ב"ן וּפָגַֽמְתִּי בְּאוֹת (י) שֶׁל שִׁמְךָ (יהוה) וּבָאוֹת (א) שֶׁל (אדני) יְהֹוָה יי נוֹעֵ[ב] לְפָנֶֽיךָ ס"ג מ"ה ב"ן כְּאִלּוּ נִסְקַֽלְתִּי בְּבֵית ב"פ ראה דִּין עַל יְדֵי אוֹת (א) שֶׁל שֵׁם (אדני). וְאָם וְחָטָֽאתִי לְפָנֶֽיךָ ס"ג מ"ה ב"ן וּפָגַֽמְתִּי בְּאוֹת (ה) רִאשׁוֹנָה שֶׁל שִׁמְךָ (יהוה) וּבָאוֹת (ד) שֶׁל (אדני) יְהֹוָה יי נוֹעֵב לְפָנֶֽיךָ ס"ג מ"ה ב"ן כְּאִלּוּ נִשְׂרַֽפְתִּי בְּבֵית ב"פ ראה דִּין עַל יְדֵי אוֹת (ד) שֶׁל שֵׁם (ו) שֶׁל שֵׁם (אדני). וְאָם וְחָטָֽאתִי לְפָנֶֽיךָ ס"ג מ"ה ב"ן וּפָגַֽמְתִּי בְּאוֹת (ו) שֶׁל שִׁמְךָ (יהוה) וּבָאוֹת (ו) שֶׁל (אדני) יְהֹוָה יי נוֹעֵב לְפָנֶֽיךָ ס"ג מ"ה ב"ן כְּאִלּוּ נֶהֱרַֽגְתִּי בַּסַּֽיִף בְּבֵית ב"פ ראה דִּין עַל יְדֵי אוֹת (ו) שֶׁל שֵׁם (אדני). וְאָם וְחָטָֽאתִי לְפָנֶֽיךָ ס"ג מ"ה ב"ן וּפָגַֽמְתִּי בְּאוֹת (ה) אַחֲרוֹנָה שֶׁל שִׁמְךָ (יהוה) וּבָאוֹת (י) שֶׁל (אדני) יְהֹוָה יי נוֹעֵב לְפָנֶֽיךָ ס"ג מ"ה ב"ן כְּאִלּוּ נֶחֱנַֽקְתִּי בְּבֵית ב"פ ראה דִּין עַל יְדֵי אוֹת (י) שֶׁל שֵׁם (אדני) (וישוב בעצמו כאילו מת על ידי בית דין)

ANA BEKO'ACH (at this point we recite the *Ana Beko'ach* – See page 55)

Recite the line that corresponds to each particular night, the start of the next day, three times.

NAFSHI IVITICHA

According to Kabbalah, death occurs for two reasons:

1) A person has accumulated so much negativity in this lifetime that he faces no possibility of transforming the nature of his current incarnation. The process of death acts as a cleansing agent that destroys the reactive nature of the body. The soul then returns in a new body to begin its spiritual work again.

2) The Ari says death also occurs when a person has attained a certain level of spirituality. He leaves this world to reincarnate and begin work toward the next level of spiritual growth.

This verse helps us to cleanse and eliminate the reactive nature of our body so that we need not go through the process of death. It allows us to continue working toward higher spiritual levels in our current incarnation.

נַפְשִׁי nafshi אִוִּיתִךָ iviticha בַּלַּיְלָה balayla מלה

אַף af רוּחִי ruchi בְּקִרְבִּי vekirbi עדי אֲשַׁחֲרֶךָּ ashachareka

כִּי ki כַּאֲשֶׁר ka'asher מִשְׁפָּטֶיךָ mishpatecha לָאָרֶץ la'aretz

צֶדֶק tzedek לָמְדוּ lamdu יֹשְׁבֵי yoshvei תֵבֵל tevel ב"פ רי"ו:

With my soul I have desired You at night, and with my spirit within me, I will seek You early in the morning. For when Your judgments are in the earth, the inhabitants of the world will learn righteousness.

Lamnatze'ach

The Ari teaches that this Psalm helps to enhance and stimulate our memory. It also helps the soul achieve its full potential in terms of motivating us to accomplish all the spiritual work that we came to this world to do.

לַמְנַצֵּחַ lamnatze'ach מִזְמוֹר mizmor לְדָוִד leDavid: בְּבוֹא bevo אֵלָיו elav

נָתָן Natan הַנָּבִיא hanavi כַּאֲשֶׁר ka'asher בָּא ba אֶל el אֲדֹנָי ; יל״ה

בַּת־שֶׁבַע Batshava: וְחָנֵּנִי choneni אֱלֹהִים Elohim אהיה אדני ; יל״ה

כְּחַסְדֶּךָ kechasdecha כְּרֹב kerov רַחֲמֶיךָ rachamecha מְחֵה meche

פְּשָׁעָי fesha'ai: הֶרֶב herev (כתיב : הַרְבֵּה) כַּבְּסֵנִי kabeseni

מֵעֲוֹנִי me'avoni וּמֵחַטָּאתִי umechatati טַהֲרֵנִי tahareni: כִּי ki פְּשָׁעַי fesha'ai

אֲנִי ani אֵדָע eda וְחַטָּאתִי vechatati נֶגְדִּי negdi נגד, מזבוח, זך, אל יהוה

תָמִיד tamid ע״ה קס״א קנ״א קמ״ג: לְךָ lecha לְבַדְּךָ levadecha וְחָטָאתִי chatati

וְהָרַע vehara עָשִׂיתִי asiti לְמַעַן lema'an בְּעֵינֶיךָ be'enecha ע״ה קס״א ; ריבוע דמ״ה

תִּצְדַּק titzdak בְּדָבְרֶךָ bedovrecha תִּזְכֶּה tizke בְשָׁפְטֶךָ veshoftecha: הֵן hen

בְּעָווֹן be'avon חוֹלָלְתִּי cholalti וּבְחֵטְא uvchet יֶחֱמַתְנִי yechematni אִמִּי imi:

To the Chief Musician, a Psalm of David, when Nathan, the prophet, came to him after he (David) had come upon Bathsheba: Have mercy upon me, God, and according to Your compassion and the multitude of Your mercies, wipe away my transgressions. Wash away my iniquities and purify me from my sins, because I acknowledge my sins and my transgressions are before me, always. I have sinned before You alone and I have done this evil before Your eyes; You are justified when you speak and are clear in Your judgment. I was born in iniquity and my mother conceived me in sin.

הֵן **hen**   **emet** אֱמֶת   אהיה פעמים אהיה, ז"פ ס"ג   **chafatzta** וְחָפַצְתָּ   **vatuchot** בַּטֻחוֹת

וּבְסָתֻם **uvsatum**   **chochmah** וְחָכְמָה   במילוי = תרי"ג (מצוות)   **todi'eni** תוֹדִיעֵנִי׃

תְּחַטְאֵנִי **techateni**   **ve'ezov** בְּאֵזוֹב   **ve'ethar** וְאֶטְהָר   **techabseni** תְּכַבְּסֵנִי

וּמִשֶּׁלֶג **umisheleg**   אלף אלף אלף (ד"ג אהיה)   **albin** אַלְבִּין׃   **tashmi'eni** תַּשְׁמִיעֵנִי

שָׂשׂוֹן **sason**   **vesimcha** וְשִׂמְחָה   **tagelna** תָּגֵלְנָה   **atzamot** עֲצָמוֹת   **dikita** דִּכִּיתָ׃

הַסְתֵּר **haster**   **mechata'ai** מֵחֲטָאַי   **panecha** פָּנֶיךָ   ס"ג מ"ה בן   מוֹזְטָאַי   **vechol** וְכָל־ יל"י

עֲוֹנֹתַי **avonotai**   מוֹזֶה **meche** ׃ **lev** לֵב   **tahor** טָהוֹר   י"פ אכא **bera** בְּרָא קנ"א ב"ן,

יהוה אלהים יהוה אדני, מילוי קס"א וס"ג, מ"ה ברבוע וע"ב ע"ה ; לב טהור ברא = קס"א קנ"א קמ"ג

לִי **li**   **Elohim** אֱלֹהִים   אהיה אדני ; ילה ; לי אלהים = ריבוע אדני   **veru'ach** וְרוּחַ

נָכוֹן **nachon**   **chadesh** וְחַדֵּשׁ   י"ב הויות, קס"א קנ"א   **bekirbi** בְּקִרְבִּי׃   עדי"י

אַל **al**   **tashlicheni** תַּשְׁלִיכֵנִי   **milfanecha** מִלְּפָנֶיךָ   ס"ג מ"ה בן

וְרוּחַ **veru'ach**   **kodshecha** קָדְשְׁךָ   **al** אַל   **tikach** תִּקַּח   **mimeni** מִמֶּנִּי׃

הָשִׁיבָה **hashiva**   **li** לִי   **seson** שְׂשׂוֹן   **yishecha** יִשְׁעֶךָ   **veru'ach** וְרוּחַ

נְדִיבָה **nediva**   **tismecheni** תִסְמְכֵנִי׃   **alameda** אֲלַמְּדָה   **fosh'im** פֹשְׁעִים

דְּרָכֶיךָ **derachecha**   **vechata'im** וְחַטָּאִים   **elecha** אֵלֶיךָ   **yashuvu** יָשׁוּבוּ׃

You desire truth and You shall inform me of the most concealed of wisdom. Purge me with hyssop and I shall be clean. Wash me and I shall be whiter than snow. Make me hear joy and gladness, so that the bones which You have broken may rejoice. Hide Your Face from my sins and wipe away all my iniquities. Create for me a pure heart and renew the correct spirit within me. Do not cast me away from Your Presence and do not withhold Your Holy Spirit from me. Restore to me the joy of Your salvation and uphold me with Your free spirit. Then I shall teach transgressors Your ways, and sinners will return to You.

הַצִּילֵנִי hatzileni מִדָּמִים midamim אֱלֹהִים Elohim אֱהֹיֶה אֲדֹנָי ; ילה

לְשׁוֹנִי leshoni תְּרַנֵּן teranen תְּשׁוּעָתִי te'shuati ; ילה, דמב, מילוי דע"ב Elohei אֱלֹהֵי

וּפִי ufi תִּפְתָּח tiftach שְׂפָתַי sefatai ללה Adonai אֲדֹנָי :tzidkatecha צִדְקָתֶךָ

כִּי ki בוכו ס"ת :tehilatecha תְּהִלָּתֶךָ (בַזְּהַר אותיות ה' (=אכא) אותיות כ"ב) ייו yagid יַגִּיד

עוֹלָה ola קמ"ג קנ"א קס"א נתה, ve'etena וְאֶתֵּנָה zevach זֶבַח tachpotz תַחְפֹּץ lo לֹא

רוּחַ ru'ach ; ילה אֲדֹנָי אֱהֹיֶה Elohim אֱלֹהִים zivchei זִבְחֵי tirtze:תִרְצֶה lo לֹא

נִשְׁבָּרָה nishbar לֵב lev (עבס"ת ס"ג בעם וימתיקם) אלהים ג'פ ר"ת nishbara נִשְׁבָּרָה

וְנִדְכֶּה venidke ר"ת אֲדֹנָי אֱהֹיֶה, אלהים Elohim אֱלֹהִים אֲדֹנָי אֱהֹיֶה ; ילה

לֹא lo תִבְזֶה tivze ר"ת ה"פ אלהים ע"ה ; ס"ת מילוי דע"ב:

הֵיטִיבָה heitiva בִרְצוֹנְךָ virtzoncha אֶת־ et צִיּוֹן Tziyon יוסף, ו' הויות, קנאה

תִבְנֶה tivne וְחוֹמוֹת chomot ע"ה קמ"ג קנ"א קס"א :Yerushalayim יְרוּשָׁלָיִם

אָז az תַחְפֹּץ tachpotz זִבְחֵי zivchei צֶדֶק tzedek עוֹלָה ola וְכָלִיל vechalil

אָז az יַעֲלוּ ya'alu עַל־ al מִזְבַּחֲךָ mizbachacha פָרִים:farim

Save me from bloodguilt, God: You are the God of my salvation. My tongue shall sing Your praise. Lord, open my lips and my heart shall say Your praise. You do not desire sacrifices and You do not want the offerings that I give. The sacrifices of God are a broken spirit and a broken and contrite heart. Do not despise, God. Improve Zion with Your good will and build the walls of Jerusalem. Then You shall be pleased with the sacrifices of righteousness: the burnt-offerings, and the whole-offerings. Then bullocks will be placed upon Your Altar.

Im Tishkav

These five verses act like a deposit on our soul, guaranteeing that it will return to us in the morning.

לֹא־ lo tishkav תִּשְׁכַּב im אִם־ יוֹהֶךְ, מ"א אותיות הפשוט, דמילוי ודמילוי דמילוי דאהיה ע"ה

תִּפְחָד tifchad veshachavta וְשָׁכַבְתָּ ve'arva וְעָרְבָה shenatecha שְׁנָתֶךָ:

אַתָּה ata seter סֵתֶר li לִי ב"פ מצר ר"ת סאל, אמן (יאהדונהי) mitzar מִצַּר מצר ; ר"ת סמאל

תִּצְּרֵנִי titzreni rane רָנֵּי falet פַלֵּט tesoveveni תְּסוֹבְבֵנִי sela סֶלָה:

תוֹדִיעֵנִי todi'eni orach אֹרַח vachayim וָחַיִּים אהיה אהיה יהוה, בינה ע"ה sova שֹׂבַע

שְׂמָחוֹת semachot et אֶת־ panecha פָּנֶיךָ ס"ג מ"ה ב"ן ne'imot נְעִמוֹת

בִּימִינְךָ bimincha netzach נֶצַח: ata אַתָּה takum תָּקוּם כ"א ההויות שבתפילין

תְרַחֵם terachem ג"פ רי"ו ; אברהם, וז"פ אל, רי"ו ול"ב נתיבות החכמה,

רמ"ו (אברים), עסמ"ב וט"ו אותיות פשוטות Tziyon צִיּוֹן יוסף, ו' הויות, קנאה ki כִּי et עֵת

לְחֶנְנָה lechenena ki כִּי va בָא mo'ed מוֹעֵד: beyadcha בְּיָדְךָ afkid אַפְקִיד

רוּחִי ruchi ר"ת קנ"א ב"ן, יהוה אלהים יהוה אדני, מילוי קס"א וס"ג, מ"ה ברבוע וע"ב ע"ה

פָּדִיתָה padita oti אוֹתִי יְהֹוָה Adonai אדניאהדונהי ר"ת פאי, אמן (יאהדונהי)

אֵל El יא"י (מילוי דס"ג) emet אֱמֶת אהיה פעמים אהיה, ז"פ ס"ג:

If you lie down, you shall not fear. You shall lie down and your sleep shall be sweet. You are my refuge. You shall shield me away from trouble. You shall surround me with songs of deliverance. Inform me about the path of life. In Your presence is fullness of joy. At Your Hand, there is pleasantness for eternity. You shall rise to have mercy over Zion, for it is time for compassion. For the time has come. In Your Hands, I entrust my spirit, for You will redeem me, Lord, true God.

BLESSINGS BEFORE FOOD

Blessing is a confusing word. Its connotations suggest that we are praising or thanking God for the food we eat. However, the truth is that God does not need or want our thanks. Nor did we come into this world to sing God's praises; we came here to become the cause and creator of our own joy, happiness and Light. To give us this opportunity, the Light (paradise) was hidden away. Our job is to find it.

Consider the case of food. If we simply eat food without reciting the blessing, the spark of Light inside the food remains dormant and inactive; all we receive from the food is nutrition, which only constitutes one percent of the food's energy. But when we recite blessings over the food we ignite the Divine spark within it, enabling us to receive both the one percent of its energy that nourishes our bodies and the 99 percent of its energy that feeds our souls.

By reciting the blessing, we become the cause of the Light's revelation in the food. Now the food not only provides nutrition but also healing, wellness and spiritual contentment. According to sixteenth-century Kabbalist Rav Isaac Luria (the Ari), a body only filled with nutrients inevitably becomes dark and spiritually weighted down. Moreover, food that is eaten without its Light being released through blessing will feed the negative forces that dwell within the body as a result of selfish, reactive behavior. When we bless the food, we ignite the Light, and any negative forces within us are deprived of nourishment.

We hold the food in our right hand and recite the blessing appropriate to the food we are about to eat.

HAMOTZI – BLESSING OVER BREAD (MADE OF WHEAT, BARLEY, RYE, OATS, OR SPELT)

Blessed are You, Lord, our God, King of the universe, Who brings forth bread from the earth.

MEZONOT – BLESSING OVER GRAINS OTHER THAN BREAD OR MATZAH

(Pastas, cake, cookies, cereals, crackers, pies, pastry, rice, etc)

יכה | Elohenu אֱלֹהֵינוּ | Adonai יְהֹוָהאדֹנָיאהדונהי | Ata אַתָּה | baruch בָּרוּךְ

mezonot מְזוֹנוֹת: | minei מִינֵי | bore בּוֹרֵא | ha'olam הָעוֹלָם | melech מֶלֶךְ

Blessed are You, Lord, our God, King of the universe, Who creates species of nourishment.

HAGEFEN – BLESSING OVER WINE OR GRAPE JUICE

יכה | Elohenu אֱלֹהֵינוּ | Adonai יְהֹוָהאדֹנָיאהדונהי | Ata אַתָּה | baruch בָּרוּךְ

hagefen הַגָּפֶן: | pri פְּרִי | bore בּוֹרֵא | ha'olam הָעוֹלָם | melech מֶלֶךְ

Blessed are You, Lord, our God, King of the universe, Creator of the fruit of the vine.

HA'ETZ – BLESSING OVER FRUITS THAT COME FROM A TREE

(Apples, pears, oranges, etc.)

(If you are unsure whether the fruit comes from a tree recite the blessing *Ha'adama* below)

יכה | Elohenu אֱלֹהֵינוּ | Adonai יְהֹוָהאדֹנָיאהדונהי | Ata אַתָּה | baruch בָּרוּךְ

ha'etz הָעֵץ: | pri פְּרִי | bore בּוֹרֵא | ha'olam הָעוֹלָם | melech מֶלֶךְ

Blessed are You, Lord, our God, King of the universe, Who creates the fruit of the tree.

HA'ADAMA – BLESSING OVER FRUITS AND VEGETABLES THAT COME FROM THE GROUND

(Strawberries, carrots, bananas, beans, etc)

יכה Elohenu אֱלֹהֵינוּ Adonai יְהֹוָאֲדֹנָיאהדונהי Ata אַתָּה baruch בָּרוּךְ

ha'adamah הָאֲדָמָה: pri פְּרִי bore בּוֹרֵא ha'olam הָעוֹלָם melech מֶלֶךְ

Blessed are You, Lord, our God, King of the universe, Who creates the fruit of the ground.

SHEHAKOL – BLESSING OVER FOODS WITH NO PARTICULAR OR DISTINGUISHABLE ORIGIN

(Dairy products, eggs, candy, meat and poultry, fish, water, drinks other than wine, etc.)

יכה Elohenu אֱלֹהֵינוּ Adonai יְהֹוָאֲדֹנָיאהדונהי Ata אַתָּה baruch בָּרוּךְ

bidvaro בִּדְבָרוֹ: nih'ya נִהְיָה shehakol שֶׁהַכֹּל ha'olam הָעוֹלָם melech מֶלֶךְ

Blessed are You, Lord, our God, King of the universe, through Whose word everything came to be.

BIRKAT HAMAZON

Birkat Hamazon - the blessing over the bread and food, is our tool to allow physical and spiritual energies to be digested and processed properly, so we can benefit this energy.

As we know food contains sparks of souls, and by this blessing we can elevate those who were in our food, and help them with their *Tikkun*.

THE FIRST BLESSING - THE WORLD OF ATZILUT/EMANATION

(On Shabbat meditate: יוד ויו דלת)

God gave sustenance to the whole world. We are now receiving the power of sustenance and prosperity. But there is one requirement: We must understand that whatever we own is merely on loan. All sustenance originates from the Creator. This awareness ensures that we keep our sustenance our entire life, thus avoiding the financial roller coaster that plagues most families. If we believe that we are the architects and providers of our own wealth, we open ourselves up to the Satan and the potential for ups and downs and loss of sustenance.

בָּרוּךְ baruch אַתָּה Ata יְהֹוָואהדונהי Adonai אֱלֹהֵינוּ Elohenu מֶלֶךְ melech

הָעוֹלָם ha'olam, הַזָּן hazan אֶת et הָעוֹלָם ha'olam כֻּלּוֹ kulo, בְּטוּבוֹ betuvo

בְּחֵן bechen בְּחֶסֶד bechesed וּבְרַחֲמִים uv'rachamim, הוּא hu נָתֵן noten

לֶחֶם lechem לְכֹל lechol בָּשָׂר basar כִּי ki לְעוֹלָם le'olam וְחַסְדּוֹ chasdo:

Blessed are you, Lord, our God, King of the Universe, who nourishes the entire world, in His goodness - with grace, with kindness and with mercy. He gives nourishment to all flesh, for His kindness is eternal.

uv'tuvo וּבְטוּבוֹ   hagadol, הַגָּדוֹל   tamid תָּמִיד   lo לֹא   chasar וְזֹסַר

lanu, לָֽנוּ   ve'al וְאַל   yechsar יֶוְזְסַר   lanu לָֽנוּ   mazon מָזוֹן

leolam לְעוֹלָם   va'ed, וָעֶד   ba'avur בַּעֲבוּר   shemo שְׁמוֹ   hagadol, הַגָּדוֹל

ki כִּי   hu הוּא   El אֵל   zan זָן   um'farnes וּמְפַרְנֵס   lakol לְכֹל

umetiv וּמֵטִיב   lakol, לַכֹּל   umechin וּמֵכִין   mazon מָזוֹן   lechol לְכָל

beriyotav בְּרִיּוֹתָיו   asher אֲשֶׁר   bara בָּרָא   ka'amur: כָּאָמוּר

And through His great goodness, we have never lacked, and may we never lack, nourishment, for all eternity. For the sake of His Great Name because He is God who nourishes and sustains all, and benefits all, and He prepares food for all His creatures which He has created. As it is said:

POTEACH ET YADECHA

We connect to the letters *Pei, Alef,* and *Yud* by opening our hands and holding our palms skyward.

Our consciousness is focused on receiving sustenance and financial prosperity from the Light through our actions of personal tithing and sharing, our Desire to Receive for the Sake of Sharing. In doing so, we also acknowledge that the sustenance we receive comes from a higher source and is not of our own doing.

According to Kabbalah, if we do not meditate on this idea at this juncture, we must repeat the prayer.

פתוז (שיע"וז נהורין לכמ"ה ולס"ה)

יוד הי ויו הי יוד הי ויו הי הי (וז' וזיוורתי)

אלף לכמד אלף לכמד (עי"ע)

יוד הא ואו הא (כו"א)

אדני (ולנוקבא)

פּוֹתֵחַ pote'ach **אֶת** et **יָדֶךָ** ר"ת פּאי וס"ת וזתך עם ג' אותיות = **דִּיקָרְנוֹסָא** yadecha

ובאתב"ע הוא סאל, פּאי, אבן, יאהדונהי ; ועוד יכוין שם וזתך בעילוב יהוה – **יוֹזֹהתוֹכֶה**

Drawing abundance and sustenance from *Chochmah* of *Ze'ir Anpin*

יוד הי ויו הי יוד הי ויו דלת הי יוד ויו יוד הי ויו יוד

וזתך סאל יאהדונהי

וּמַשְׂבִּיעַ umasbi'a וזתך עם ג' אותיות = **דִּיקָרְנוֹסָא**

ובא"ת ב"ע הוא סאל, אבן, יאהדונהי ; ועוד יכוין שם וזתך בעילוב יהוה – **יוֹזֹהתוֹכֶה**

Drawing abundance and sustenance from *Chochmah* of *Ze'ir Anpin*

יוד הי ויו הי יוד הי ויו דלת הי יוד ויו יוד הי ויו יוד

לְכָל־ lechol יה אדני (להמשיך מווזין ד–יה אל הנוקבא שהיא אדני)

רָצוֹן ratzon מוהש ע"ה, ע"ב ברבוע וקס"א ע"ה, אל שדי ע"ה

ר"ת רוזל שהיא המלכות הצריכה לשפע

יוד יוד הי יוד הי ויו יוד הי ויו הי ויו הי יסוד דאבא אלף הי יוד הי יסוד דאימא

להמתיק רוזל וב' רמעין **עֹךְ פּר**

בָּרוּךְ baruch **אַתָּה** atah **הַזָּן** Adonai hazan **אֶת** et **הַכֹּל** hakol:

"You open Your hand, and satisfy the desire of every living thing. Blessed are you, Lord who nourishes all.

THE SECOND BLESSING - THE WORLD OF BERI'AH/CREATION

(On Shabbat meditate: הי יוד)

נוֹדֶה nodeh לְךָ lecha יְהֹוָאדֹנָיאהדוּנָהי Adonai אֱלֹהֵינוּ Elohenu עַל al

שֶׁהִנְחַלְתָּ shehin'chalta לַאֲבוֹתֵינוּ la'avotenu, אֶרֶץ eretz וַחֶמְדָּה chemdah

טוֹבָה tova וּרְוָחָה urchava, וְעַל veal שֶׁהוֹצֵאתָנוּ shehotzetanu

יְהֹוָאדֹנָיאהדוּנָהי Adonai אֱלֹהֵינוּ Elohenu מֵאֶרֶץ me'eretz מִצְרַיִם Mitzrayim,

וּפְדִיתָנוּ uf'ditanu מִבֵּית mibet עֲבָדִים avadim, וְעַל ve'al בְּרִיתְךָ beritcha

שֶׁחָתַמְתָּ shechatamta בִּבְשָׂרֵנוּ bivsarenu, וְעַל ve'al תּוֹרָתְךָ toratcha

שֶׁלִּמַּדְתָּנוּ shelimadetanu, וְעַל ve'al וְחֻקֶּיךָ chukecha

שֶׁהוֹדַעְתָּנוּ shehoda'atanu, וְעַל ve'al וְחַיִּים chayim וְחֵן chen וָחֶסֶד vachesed

שֶׁחוֹנַנְתָּנוּ shechonantanu, וְעַל ve'al אֲכִילַת achilat מָזוֹן mazon

שָׁאַתָּה she'atah זָן zan וּמְפַרְנֵס umfarnes אוֹתָנוּ otanu תָּמִיד tamid,

בְּכָל bechol יוֹם yom וּבְכָל uvechol עֵת et וּבְכָל uvechol שָׁעָה sha'ah:

We thank you, Lord, our God, because You have given to our forefathers as a heritage a desirable, good and spacious land; because You removed us, Lord, our God, from the land of Egypt and You redeemed us from the house of bondage; for Your covenant which You sealed in our flesh; for Your Torah which You taught us and for Your statutes which You made known to us; for life, grace and loving kindness which You granted us; and for the provision of food with which You nourish and sustain us constantly, in every day, in every season and in every hour.

CHANUKAH AND PURIM

These events generate an added dimension of the energy of miracles. This blessing helps us harness that power so that we can draw miracles into our life whenever they are truly needed.

ve'al וְעַל　hanisim הַנִּסִים　ve'al וְעַל　hapurkan הַפֻּרְקָן◆

ve'al וְעַל　hagevurot הַגְּבוּרוֹת◆　ve'al וְעַל　hateshu'ot הַתְּשׁוּעוֹת

ve'al וְעַל　hanifla'ot הַנִּפְלָאוֹת　ve'al וְעַל　hanechamot הַנֶּחָמוֹת

she'asita שֶׁעָשִׂיתָ　la'avoteinu לַאֲבוֹתֵינוּ　bayamim בַּיָּמִים　hahem הָהֵם נלך　bazeman בַּזְּמַן　haze הַזֶּה והו:

FOR CHANUKAH

bimei בִּימֵי　Matitya מַתִּתְיָה　ven בֶּן　Yochanan יוֹחָנָן　kohen כֹּהֵן מלה

gadol גָּדוֹל להוו ; עם ד' אותיות = מבה, יזל, אום　Chashmonai וְחַשְׁמוֹנָאִי　uvanav וּבָנָיו

keshe'amda כְּשֶׁעָמְדָה　malchut מַלְכוּת　Yavan יָוָן　harsha'a הָרְשָׁעָה　al עַל

amcha עַמְּךָ　Yisrael יִשְׂרָאֵל　leshakcham לְשַׁכְּחָם　toratach תּוֹרָתֶךָ

ulha'aviram וּלְהַעֲבִירָם　mechukei מֵחֻקֵּי　retzonach רְצוֹנֶךָ◆　ve'ata וְאַתָּה

verachameicha בְּרַחֲמֶיךָ　harabim הָרַבִּים　amadeta עָמַדְתָּ　lahem לָהֶם

be'et בְּעֵת　tzaratam צָרָתָם◆　ravta רַבְתָּ et אֶת　rivam רִיבָם◆　danta דַּנְתָּ et אֶת

dinam דִּינָם◆　nakamta נָקַמְתָּ מנק　et אֶת　nikmatam נִקְמָתָם מנק◆

*And also for the miracles, deliverance, the mighty acts, the salvation, wonders,
and comforting deeds that You have performed for our forefathers, in those days and at this time.*

*In the days of Matityahu, the son of Yochanan, The High Priest, The Chashmonai and his sons,
when the evil Greek Empire rose up against Your nation, Israel, to force them to forget Your Torah
and to force them away from the laws of Your desire, You, with Your compassion,
stood up for them, in their time of trouble. You fought their battles, sought justice for them, avenged them,*

וְחַלָּשִׁים chalashim •   בְּיַד beyad   גִּבּוֹרִים giborim   מָסַרְתָּ masarta

בְּיַד beyad   וּרְשָׁעִים urshaim   מְעַטִּים me'atim •   בְּיַד beyad   וְרַבִּים verabim

טְהוֹרִים tehorim •   בְּיַד beyad   וּטְמֵאִים utmeim   צַדִּיקִים tzadikim •

לְךָ lecha   תּוֹרָתֶךָ toratecha •   עוֹסְקֵי oskei   בְּיַד beyad   וְזֵדִים vezedim

עָשִׂיתָ asita   שֵׁם shem   גָּדוֹל gadol ; לְהוּ = עם ד' אותיות = מ:בה, יו:ל, אום

יִשְׂרָאֵל Yisrael   וּלְעַמְּךָ ulamcha   בְּעוֹלָמָךְ be'olamach •   וְקָדוֹשׁ vekadosh

וּפוּרְקָן ufurkan   גְּדוֹלָה gedola   תְּשׁוּעָה teshu'a   עָשִׂיתָ asita

כָּךְ kach   וְאַחַר ve'achar • והו ...   הַזֶּה haze   כְּהַיּוֹם kehayom

בֵּיתֶךָ beitecha   לִדְבִיר lidvir   בָנֶיךָ vaneicha   בָּאוּ bau

אֶת et   וְטִהֲרוּ vetiharu   הֵיכָלֶךָ heichalecha •   אֶת et   וּפִנּוּ ufinu

בְּחַצְרוֹת bechatzrot   נֵרוֹת nerot   וְהִדְלִיקוּ vehidliku   מִקְדָּשֶׁךָ mikdashecha •

וְזֻנְכָּה chanuka   יְמֵי yemei   שְׁמוֹנַת shemonat   וְקָבְעוּ vekavu   קָדְשֶׁךָ kodshecha •

וְעָשִׂיתָ ve'asita   וּבְהוֹדָאָה uvehoda'a •   בְּהַלֵּל behalel   אֵלּוּ elu

לְשִׁמְךָ leshimcha   וְנוֹדֶה venode   וְנִפְלָאוֹת veniflaot   נִסִּים nisim   עִמָּהֶם imahem

סֶלָה sela :   לְהוּ = מ:בה, יו:ל, אום   הַגָּדוֹל hagadol

---

and delivered the strong into the hands of the weak, the many into the hands of the few, the wicked into the hands of the righteous, the defiled into the hands of the pure. And the tyrants into the hands of those who occupy themselves with Your Torah. For Yourself, You made a Holy Name in Your world, and for Your people, Israel, You carried out a great salvation and deliverance on this day. Then, Your children came into the Sanctuary of Your House, they cleansed Your Palace, they purified Your Temple, they lit candles in the courtyards of Your Holy domain, and they instituted those eight days of Chanukah for praise and thanksgiving. And You performed for them miracles and wonders. For that, we are grateful to Your great Name, Selah!

For Purim:

עִם הָאוֹתִיּוֹת = מִילוּי אֲדֹנָי veEster וְאֶסְתֵּר Mardechai מָרְדְּכַי bimei בִּימֵי

aleihem עֲלֵיהֶם keshe'amad כְּשֶׁעָמַד habira. הַבִּירָה beShushan בְּשׁוּשַׁן

laharog לַהֲרוֹג lehashmid לְהַשְׁמִיד bikesh בִּקֵּשׁ harasha. הָרָשָׁע Haman הָמָן

ve'ad וְעַד mina'ar מִנַּעַר hayehudim הַיְּהוּדִים kol כָּל et אֶת ulabed וּלְאַבֵּד

ע"ה נגד, מוזבו, זן, אל יהוה beyom בְּיוֹם venashim וְנָשִׁים taf טַף zaken זָקֵן

lechodesh לְוֹדֶשׁ asar עָשָׂר bishlsha בִּשְׁלֹשָׁה דאגה אהבה, echad אֶחָד

י"ב הויות, קס"א קנ"א chodesh וֹדֶשׁ hu הוּא asar עָשָׂר sheneim שְׁנֵים קס"א קנ"א

verachameicha בְּרַחֲמֶיךָ ve'ata וְאַתָּה lavoz לָבוֹז ushlalam וּשְׁלָלָם adar אֲדָר

vekilkalta וְקִלְקַלְתָּ atzato עֲצָתוֹ et אֶת hefarta הֵפַרְתָּ harabim הָרַבִּים

gemulo גְּמוּלוֹ lo לוֹ vahashevota וַהֲשֵׁבוֹתָ machashavto. מַחֲשַׁבְתּוֹ et אֶת

ha'etz. הָעֵץ al עַל banav בָּנָיו ve'et וְאֶת oto אוֹתוֹ vetalu וְתָלוּ berosho. בְּרֹאשׁוֹ

venode וְנוֹדֶה venifla'ot וְנִפְלָאוֹת nisim נִסִּים imahem עִמָּהֶם ve'asita וְעָשִׂיתָ

sela: סֶלָה להו ; עם ד' אותיות = מבה, זל, אום hagadol הַגָּדוֹל leshimcha לְשִׁמְךָ

In the days of Mordechai and Esther, in Shushan, the capital, when the evil Haman rose up against them - he sought to destroy, slay, and annihilate all the Jews, young and old, children and women, in one day, on the thirteenth day of the twelfth month, which is the month of Adar, and to take their spoils - but You, in Your great compassion, ruined his plan, foiled his design, and turned his due upon his own head. They hanged him and his sons upon the gallows. And You performed for them [Israel] miracles and wonders. We give thanks to Your great Name, Selah!

ve'al **וְעַל**   hakol **הַכֹּל**   Adonai **יהוה**   Elohenu **אֱלֹהֵינוּ**

anachnu **אֲנַחְנוּ**   modim **מוֹדִים**   lach **לָךְ,**   umevarchim **וּמְבָרְכִים**   otach **אוֹתָךְ,**

yitbarach **יִתְבָּרַךְ**   shimcha **שִׁמְךָ**   befi **בְּפִי**   kol **כָּל**   chai **חַי**

tamid **תָּמִיד**   le'olam **לְעוֹלָם**   va'ed **וָעֶד.**   kakatuv **כַּכָּתוּב:**

vachalta **וְאָכַלְתָּ**   vesavata **וְשָׂבָעְתָּ**   uverachta **וּבֵרַכְתָּ**   et **אֶת**

hatova **הַטֹּבָה**   ha'aretz **הָאָרֶץ**   al **עַל**   Elohecha **אֱלֹהֶיךָ**   Adonai **יהוה**

atah **אַתָּה**   baruch **בָּרוּךְ**   lach **לָךְ:**   natan **נָתַן**   asher **אֲשֶׁר**

hamazon **הַמָּזוֹן:**   ve'al **וְעַל**   ha'aretz **הָאָרֶץ**   al **עַל**   Adonai **יהוה**

For all, Lord, our God, we thank You and bless You. May Your name be blessed by the mouth of all the living, continuously for all eternity. As it is written: "And you shall eat and you shall be satisfied and you shall bless Lord, your God for the good land which He gave you. Blessed are you, Lord, for the land and the nourishment.

THE THIRD BLESSING - THE WORLD OF YETZIRAH/FORMATION

(On Shabbat meditate: ויו יוד ויו)

Have Mercy on Israel.

The word *Rachem* (mercy) has a numerical value of 248, the same numerical value as the name *Avraham.* Abraham was known for having constant mercy for all people. 248 is also the number of spiritual and physical body parts of an individual. A surefire method for generating healing energy for all the 248 parts of our body is behaving with mercy toward others, as Abraham did. This blessing is our drawbridge to the Upper Worlds, bringing the healing Light to each of our body parts. When we live our lives with mercy toward others, the bridge is down and the energy flows. When we behave otherwise, the bridge is drawn, cutting off the flow of energy.

רַחֵם rachem נָא na יְהֹוָה/אֲדֹנָי Adonai אֱלֹהֵינוּ Elohenu, עַל al

יִשְׂרָאֵל Yisrael עַמֶּךָ amecha, וְעַל ve'al יְרוּשָׁלַיִם Yerushalayim

עִירֶךָ irecha, וְעַל ve'al צִיּוֹן Tzion מִשְׁכַּן mishkan כְּבוֹדֶךָ kevodecha,

וְעַל ve'al מַלְכוּת malchut בֵּית bet דָּוִד David מְשִׁיחֶךָ meshichecha,

וְעַל ve'al הַבַּיִת habayit הַגָּדוֹל hagadol וְהַקָּדוֹשׁ vehakadosh

שֶׁנִּקְרָא shenikra שִׁמְךָ shimcha עָלָיו alav. אֱלֹהֵינוּ Elohenu, אָבִינוּ avinu,

רְעֵנוּ re'enu, זוּנֵנוּ zunenu פַּרְנְסֵנוּ parnesenu וְכַלְכְּלֵנוּ vechalkelenu,

וְהַרְוִיחֵנוּ veharvichenu, וְהַרְוַח veharvach לָנוּ lanu יְהֹוָה/אֲדֹנָי Adonai

אֱלֹהֵינוּ Elohenu מְהֵרָה meherah מִכָּל mikol צָרוֹתֵינוּ tzarotenu. וְנָא vena,

אַל al תַּצְרִיכֵנוּ tatzrichenu יְהֹוָה/אֲדֹנָי Adonai אֱלֹהֵינוּ Elohenu,

לֹא lo לִידֵי lide וְלֹא velo וָדָם vadam בָּשָׂר basar מַתְּנַת matenat לִידֵי lide

הַלְוָאָתָם halva'atam. כִּי ki אִם im לְיָדְךָ leyadecha הַמְּלֵאָה hamele'a,

הַפְּתוּחָה hapetucha, הַקְּדוֹשָׁה hakedosha וְהָרְחָבָה veharechava, שֶׁלֹא shelo

נֵבוֹשׁ nevosh וְלֹא velo נִכָּלֵם nikalem לְעוֹלָם le'olam וָעֶד va'ed.

Have mercy, please Lord, our God, on Israel Your people; on Jerusalem, Your city, on Zion, the resting place of Your glory; on the monarchy of the house of David Your anointed; and on the great and holy house upon which Your Name is called. Our God, our Father — tend us, nourish us, sustain us support us, relieve us; Lord, our God, grant us speedy relief from all our troubles. Please, make us not needful — Lord our God — of the gifts of human hands nor of their loans, but only of Your hand that is full, open, holy an generous, that we not feel inner shame nor be humiliated for ever and ever.

For Shabbat:

In Birkat HaMazon, in order to make the connection to the energy od Shabbat in the the third blessing we are adding "Retze Vehachalitzenu". The third blessing correlates to the realm of Zeir Anpin, the dimension and source for all the spiritual Light that flows into our realm.

Also the word "Hachalitzenu" means – release us - the third blessing correlates to the World of formation which, during the weekdays, is ruled by The Angel Matat-ron (do not pronounce), and on Shabbat we would like to be disconnected from it and be elevated to higher dimensions (the World of Atziut and higher).

retze רְצֵה   vehachalitzenu וְהַחֲלִיצֵנוּ   Adonai יְהוָֹאדְנִיַאהדוֹנָהי   Elohenu אֱלֹהֵינוּ

bemitzvotecha בְּמִצְוֹתֶיךָ   uv'mitzvat וּבְמִצְוַת   yom יוֹם   hashevi'i, הַשְּׁבִיעִי

haShabbat הַשַּׁבָּת   hagadol הַגָּדוֹל   vehakadosh וְהַקָּדוֹשׁ   hazeh הַזֶּה.

ki כִּי   yom יוֹם   ze זֶה   gadol גָּדוֹל   vekadosh וְקָדוֹשׁ   hu הוּא   lefanecha, לְפָנֶיךָ

lishbot לִשְׁבָּת   bo בּוֹ   velanu'ach וְלָנוּחַ   bo בּוֹ   be'ahava בְּאַהֲבָה

lanu לָנוּ   kemitzvat כְּמִצְוֹת   retzonecha רְצוֹנֶךָ.   uvirtzoncha וּבִרְצוֹנְךָ   hani'ach הָנִיחַ

tehe תְּהֵא   tzara צָרָה   veyagon וְיָגוֹן   va'anachah וַאֲנָחָה   beyom בְּיוֹם

menuchatenu מְנוּחָתֵנוּ.   vehar'enu וְהַרְאֵנוּ   Adonai יְהוָֹאדְנִיַאהדוֹנָהי   Elohenu אֱלֹהֵינוּ

benechamat בְּנֶחָמַת   Tzion צִיּוֹן   irecha, עִירֶךָ   uvevinyan וּבְבִנְיַן

Yerushalayim יְרוּשָׁלַיִם   ir עִיר   kodshecha, קָדְשֶׁךָ   ki כִּי   ata אַתָּה

hu הוּא   ba'al בַּעַל   hayeshu'ot הַיְשׁוּעוֹת   uva'al וּבַעַל   hane'chamot הַנֶּחָמוֹת:

May it please You, Lord, our God – give us rest through Your commandments of the Seventh Day, this great and holy Shbbath. For this day is great and holy before You to rest on it and be content on it in love, as ordained by Your will. May it be Your will, Lord, our God, that there be no distress, grief or lament on this day of our contentment. And show us, Lord, our God, the consolation of Zion, Your city, and the rebuilding of Jerusalem, city of Your holiness, for You are the Master of salvation and Master of consolations.

ON ROSH CHODESH (BEGINNING OF A NEW LUNAR MONTH) AND HOLIDAYS:

During these events,
we find an extra surge of spiritual energy in our midst. We have an additional blessing that is our antenna for drawing this extra power.

veyavo וְיָבֹא   ya'aleh יַעֲלֶה   avotenu אֲבוֹתֵינוּ   velohe וֵאלֹהֵי   Elohenu אֱלֹהֵינוּ

veyipaked וְיִפָּקֵד   veyishama וְיִשָּׁמַע   veyeratze וְיֵרָצֶה   veyera'e וְיֵרָאֶה   veyagi'a וְיַגִּיעַ

•avotenu אֲבוֹתֵינוּ   vezichron וְזִכְרוֹן   zichronenu זִכְרוֹנֵנוּ   veyizacher וְיִזָּכֵר

vezichron וְזִכְרוֹן   •irach עִירָךְ   Yerushalayim יְרוּשָׁלַיִם   zichron זִכְרוֹן

kol כָּל   vezichron וְזִכְרוֹן   •avdach עַבְדָּךְ   David דָּוִד   ben בֶּן   Mashi'ach מְשִׁיחַ

lifleta לִפְלֵיטָה   lefanecha לְפָנֶיךָ   Yisrael יִשְׂרָאֵל   bet בֵּית   amcha עַמְּךָ

•ulerachamim וּלְרַחֲמִים   lechesed לְחֶסֶד   lechen לְחֵן   •letova לְטוֹבָה

:beyom בְּיוֹם   •uleshalom וּלְשָׁלוֹם   tovim טוֹבִים   lechayim לְחַיִּים

•haze הַזֶּה   hachodesh הַחֹדֶשׁ   rosh רֹאשׁ   :   On   Rosh   Chodesh

•haze הַזֶּה   haMatzot הַמַּצּוֹת   chag חַג   :   On   Pesach

•haze הַזֶּה   kodesh קֹדֶשׁ   mikra מִקְרָא   (tov טוֹב :on holiday add)   beyom בְּיוֹם

•haze הַזֶּה   haSukkot הַסֻּכּוֹת   chag חַג   :   On   Sukkot

•haze הַזֶּה   kodesh קֹדֶשׁ   mikra מִקְרָא   (tov טוֹב :on holiday add)   beyom בְּיוֹם

God and the God of our forefathers, may there rise, come, reach, be noted, be favored, be heard, be considered, and be remembered — the remembrance and consideration of ourselves; the remembrance of our forefathers; the remembrance of Messiah, son of David, Your servant; the remembrance of Jerusalem, the city of Your holiness, the remembrance of Your entire people the family of Israel — before You for deliverance, for goodness, for grace, for kindness and for compassion, for (good) life and for peace on this day of :

On Rosh Chodesh: *This Rosh Chodesh*

On Pesach: *This festival of Matzot, on this day of holy convocation.*

On Sukkot: *This holiday of Sukkot, on this day of holy convocation.*

On Shemini Atzeret : שְׁמִינִי shemini וַזֹג chag הָעֲצֶרֶת haAtzeret הַזֶּה haze•

beyom בְּיוֹם tov טוֹב mikra מִקְרָא kodesh קֹדֶשׁ הַזֶּה haze•

On Shavout : וַזֹג chag הַשָּׁבוּעוֹת haShavo'ut הַזֶּה haze•

beyom בְּיוֹם tov טוֹב mikra מִקְרָא kodesh קֹדֶשׁ הַזֶּה haze•

on Rosh Hashanah : הַזִּכָּרוֹן haZikaron הַזֶּה haze•

Children eating on Yom Kippur : הַכִּפֻּרִים haKippurim הַזֶּה haze•

lerachem לְרַחֵם bo בּוֹ alenu עָלֵינוּ וּלְהוֹשִׁיעֵנוּ ulehoshi'enu• זָכְרֵנוּ zochrenu

Adonai יְהֹוָאֲדֹנָי Elohenu אֱלֹהֵינוּ bo בּוֹ l'tovah לְטוֹבָה (amen) (אמן)•

ufokdenu וּפָקְדֵנוּ vo בּוֹ livrachah לִבְרָכָה• (amen) (אמן)•

v'hoshi'enu וְהוֹשִׁיעֵנוּ vo בּוֹ l'chayim לְחַיִּים tovim טוֹבִים• (amen) (אמן)•

bidvar בִּדְבַר yeshu'a יְשׁוּעָה v'rachamim וְרַחֲמִים chus וְחֻס

v'chonenu וְחָנֵּנוּ vachamol וַחֲמוֹל v'rachem וְרַחֵם alenu עָלֵינוּ

v'hoshienu וְהוֹשִׁיעֵנוּ ki כִּי elecha אֵלֶיךָ enenu• עֵינֵינוּ

ki כִּי el אֵל melech מֶלֶךְ chanun חַנּוּן v'rachum וְרַחוּם atah: אָתָּה

On Shemini Atzeret: *Shmini Atzeret this holiday, on this day of holy convocation.*
On Shavout: *This holiday of Shavout, on this day of holy convocation.*
On Rosh Hashanah: *This remembrance Day*
Children eating of Yom Kippur: *This Kippurim*

Remember us on it, Lord, our God, for goodness; consider us on it for blessing; and help us on it for good life. In the matter of salvation and compassion, pity, be gracious and compassionate with us and help us, for our eyes are turned to You, because You are God, the gracious and compassionate King.

UVNEH YERUSHALAYIM

The third blessing ends with the verse *Jerusalem will be built with mercy.*

The reason the Temple of Jerusalem was destroyed some 2,000 years ago was due to *Hatred for Reason.* This kind of hatred epitomizes a complete lack of mercy and tolerance between one person and another. The only way the Temple will be rebuilt, physically, is through the power of *Love for No Reason*-meaning unconditional mercy and human dignity toward our friends and enemies.

Interestingly, Kabbalah teaches us that the Temple already exists spiritually. We can bring it into physical manifestation by virtue of our unconditional love for others. Each year the Temple does not appear, it's as though we have destroyed it all over again. It is this destruction that brings about all the chaos in our world.

bimhera בִּמְהֵרָה hakodesh הַקֹּדֶשׁ ir עִיר Yerushalayim יְרוּשָׁלַיִם uvene וּבְנֵה

Adonai יְהֹוָאדֹנָיאהדונהי ata אַתָּה baruch בָּרוּךְ ◆veyamenu בְיָמֵינוּ

:amen אָמֵן ◆Yerushalayim יְרוּשָׁלַיִם verachamav בְּרַחֲמָיו bone בּוֹנֵה

May You rebuild Jerusalem,
the holy city, soon and in our days. We praise You, God, Who in mercy rebuilds Jerusalem. Amen.

THE FOURTH BLESSING-THE WORLD OF ASIYAH/ACTION

(On Shabbat meditate: הֵי יוד)

Hatov V'hametiv-All the good that God has done, is doing, and will do for us. This blessing means that whatever God gives us is what we need and not necessarily what we might want. If we are missing anything in our life, it means we are not supposed to have it. We should always try to receive everything that life can offer us, but we should not allow ourselves to be controlled by the outcome of our efforts to receive. We must learn to fully appreciate and be completely happy with all that we have in the present and not focus our efforts on attaining the next level of success as a condition for our happiness.

melech מֶלֶךְ Elohenu אֱלֹהֵינוּ Adonai יְהֹוָה ata אַתָּה baruch בָּרוּךְ

adirenu אַדִירֵנוּ, malkenu מַלְכֵּנוּ, avinu אָבִינוּ haEl הָאֵל ha'olam הָעוֹלָם,

kedoshenu קְדוֹשֵׁנוּ, yotzrenu יוֹצְרֵנוּ, go'alenu גּוֹאֲלֵנוּ, bor'enu בּוֹרְאֵנוּ,

Yisrael יִשְׂרָאֵל. ro'eh רוֹעֶה ro'enu רוֹעֵנוּ, Yaakov יַעֲקֹב kedosh קָדוֹשׁ

lakol לַכֹּל, vehametiv וְהַמֵּטִיב, hatov הַטּוֹב hamelech הַמֶּלֶךְ

hu הוּא, hetiv הֵטִיב hu הוּא vayom וָיוֹם yom יוֹם shebechol שֶׁבְּכָל

gemalanu גְּמָלָנוּ, hu הוּא lanu לָנוּ. yetiv יֵיטִיב hu הוּא, metiv מֵטִיב

la'ad לָעַד yigmelenu יִגְמְלֵנוּ hu הוּא, gomelenu גּוֹמְלֵנוּ hu הוּא

ulerevach וּלְרֶוַח, ulerachamim וּלְרַחֲמִים ulechesed וּלְחֶסֶד lechen לְחֵן

vishu'a וִישׁוּעָה, beracha בְּרָכָה vehatzlacha וְהַצְלָחָה, hatzala הַצָּלָה

verachamim וְרַחֲמִים, vechalkala וְכַלְכָּלָה parnasa פַּרְנָסָה, nechama נֶחָמָה,

tuv טוֹב, vechol וְכָל veshalom וְשָׁלוֹם, vechayim וְחַיִּים

yechasrenu יְחַסְּרֵנוּ. al אַל le'olam לְעוֹלָם tuv טוֹב umikol וּמִכָּל

Blessed are you, Lord, our God, King of the Universe, the Almighty, our Father, our King. Our Sovereign, our Creator, our Redeemer, our Maker, our Holy One, Holy one of Jacob, our Shepherd, the Shepherd of Israel, the King who is good and who does good for all. For every single day He did good, He does good and He will do good to us. He was bountiful with us, He is bountiful with us and He will forever be bountiful with us — with grace and with kindness and with mercy, with relief, salvation, success, blessing, help, consolation, sustenance, support, mercy, life, peace and all good; and of all good things may he never deprives us.

HARACHAMAN

In these next blessings, we will ask God for everything – health, happiness, sustenance, the final redemption. You name it, we're asking for it. The Kabbalists ask what the point is in praying for anything. Either God has it in the cards for us to receive, or he doesn't. The reason for asking has to do with ego, which is the only stumbling block to receiving any form of lasting fulfillment. If a person can't admit to himself that he needs God, then he can never receive Light. No matter how many positive actions we do, no matter how smart we are, without admitting and recognizing the need for the Light of the Creator, we can never receive permanent fulfillment.

הָרַחֲמָן, harachaman

הוּא hu יִמְלֹךְ yimloch עָלֵינוּ alenu לְעוֹלָם leolam וָעֶד va'ed◆

הָרַחֲמָן, harachaman

הוּא hu יִתְבָּרַךְ yitbarech בַּשָּׁמַיִם bashamayim וּבָאָרֶץ uva'aretz◆

הָרַחֲמָן, harachaman הוּא hu יִשְׁתַּבַּח yishtabach לְדוֹר ledor דּוֹרִים dorim,

וְיִתְפָּאַר veyitpa'ar בָּנוּ banu לָעַד la'ad וּלְנֵצַח ulnetzach נְצָחִים netzachim,

וְיִתְהַדַּר veyit'hadar בָּנוּ banu לָעַד la'ad וּלְעוֹלְמֵי uleolme עוֹלָמִים olamim◆

הָרַחֲמָן, harachaman הוּא hu יְפַרְנְסֵנוּ yefarnsenu בְּכָבוֹד vechavod◆

The compassionate One! May He reign over us forever. The compassionate One! May He be blessed in heaven and on earth. The compassionate One! May He be praised throughout all generations, may He be glorified through us forever to the ultimate ends, and be honored through us forever and for all eternity. The compassionate One! May He sustain us in honor.

הָרַחֲמָן, harachaman,

הוּא hu   יִשְׁבֹּר yishbor   עָלֵנוּ ulenu   מֵעַל me'al   צַוָּארֵנוּ tzavarenu

וְהוּא vehu   יוֹלִיכֵנוּ yolichenu   קוֹמְמִיּוּת komemiyut   לְאַרְצֵנוּ le'artzenu ◆

הָרַחֲמָן harachaman, הוּא hu

יִשְׁלַח yishlach   לָנוּ lanu   בְּרָכָה beracha   מְרֻבָּה meruba   בַּבַּיִת babait

הַזֶּה haze   וְעַל ve'al   שֻׁלְחָן shulchan   זֶה ze   שֶׁאָכַלְנוּ she'achalnu   עָלָיו alav ◆

הָרַחֲמָן harachaman, הוּא hu   יִשְׁלַח yishlach   לָנוּ lanu   אֶת et   אֵלִיָּהוּ Eliyahu

הַנָּבִיא hanavi   זָכוּר zachur   לַטּוֹב latov   (3x   וִיבַשֶּׂר vivaser   לָנוּ lanu)

בְּשׂוֹרוֹת besorot   טוֹבוֹת tovot   יְשׁוּעוֹת yeshu'ot   וְנֶחָמוֹת venechamot ◆

הָרַחֲמָן, harachaman,

הוּא hu   יְבָרֵךְ yevarech   אֶת et   הָרַב haRav   רַבִּי rabi   מוֹרִי mori   בַּעַל ba'al

הַבַּיִת habayit   הַזֶּה haze, וְאֶת ve'et   הָרַבָּנִית haRabanit   מוֹרָתִי morati

בַּעֲלַת ba'alat   הַבַּיִת habayit   הַזֶּה haze ◆   אוֹתָם otam   וְאֶת ve'et   בֵּיתָם betam

וְאֶת ve'et   זַרְעָם zar'am   וְאֶת ve'et   כָּל kol   אֲשֶׁר asher   לָהֶם lahem ◆

The compassionate One! May He break the yoke of oppression from our necks and guide us erect to our land. The compassionate One! May He send us abundant blessing to this house and upon this table at which we have eaten. The compassionate One! May he send us Elijah the prophet – he is remembered for good – to proclaim to us good tidings, salvations and consolations. The compassionate One! May He bless my rabbi, my teacher, the master of this house and my rebbetzin, my teacher, the lady of this house; them, their house, their family and all that is theirs.

At your table say:

(ve'imi וְאִמִּי ve'avi וְאָבִי) oti אוֹתִי yevarech יְבָרֵךְ hu הוּא, harachaman הָרַחֲמָן

ve'ishti וְאִשְׁתִּי vezar'i וְזַרְעִי ve'et וְאֶת kol כֹּל asher אֲשֶׁר li לִי.

mekomotam בִּמְקוֹמוֹתָם bechol בְּכֹל hachaverim הַחֲבֵרִים kol כֹּל ve'et וְאֶת

ve'et וְאֶת zar'am זַרְעָם ve'et וְאֶת betam בֵּיתָם ve'et וְאֶת otam אוֹתָם

asher אֲשֶׁר kol כֹּל ve'et וְאֶת otanu אוֹתָנוּ lahem לָהֶם asher אֲשֶׁר kol כֹּל

avotenu אֲבוֹתֵינוּ shenitbarchu שֶׁנִּתְבָּרְכוּ kemo כְּמוֹ, lanu לָנוּ

bakol בַּכֹּל, veYaakov וְיַעֲקֹב: Yitzchak יִצְחָק Avraham אַבְרָהָם

kulanu כֻּלָּנוּ otanu אוֹתָנוּ yevarech יְבָרֵךְ ken כֵּן kol כֹּל, mikol מִכֹּל,

amen אָמֵן: venomar וְנֹאמַר, shelema שְׁלֵמָה bivracha בִּבְרָכָה, yachad יַחַד

ve'alenu וְעָלֵינוּ alehem עֲלֵיהֶם yelamdu יְלַמְּדוּ bamarom בַּמָּרוֹם

shalom שָׁלוֹם, lemishmeret לְמִשְׁמֶרֶת shetehe שֶׁתְּהֵא, zechut זְכוּת

Adonai יְהֹוָה me'et מֵאֵת beracha בְּרָכָה venisa וְנִשָּׂא

chen חֵן venimtza וְנִמְצָא, yish'enu יִשְׁעֵנוּ meElohe מֵאֱלֹהֵי utzedakah וּצְדָקָה

ve'adam וְאָדָם Elohim אֱלֹהִים be'ene בְּעֵינֵי tov טוֹב vesechel וְשֵׂכֶל.

(Ours and all that is ours) just as our forefathers Avraham, Yitzchak and Ya'akov were blessed in everything, from everything, with everything. So may He bless us all together with a perfect blessing. And let us say: Amen On high, may merit be pleaded upon them and upon us, for a safeguard of peace. May we receive a blessing from the Lord and just kindness from the God of our salvation and find favor and good understanding in the eyes of God and man.

During the blessing for Circumcision we recite the following

Chesed   harachaman, הָרַחֲמָן   חסד

veyizku וְיִזְכּוּ, ve'imo וְאִמּוֹ hayeled הַיֶּלֶד avi אֲבִי et אֶת yevarech יְבָרֵךְ hu הוּא

miyom מִיּוֹם, ulechakemo וּלְחַכְּמוֹ ulechanecho וּלְחַנְּכוֹ legadlo לְגַדְּלוֹ

damo דָּמוֹ, yeratze יֵרָצֶה vahal'a וָהָלְאָה hashemini הַשְּׁמִינִי

(amen אָמֵן) imo עִמּוֹ Elohav אֱלֹהָיו Adonai יְדֹוָד vihi וִיהִי

Gevurah   גבורה

berit בְּרִית ba'al בַּעַל yevarech יְבָרֵךְ hu הוּא harachaman, הָרַחֲמָן

begila בְּגִילָה, tzedek צֶדֶק la'asot לַעֲשׂוֹת sas שָׂשׂ asher אֲשֶׁר hamila הַמִּילָה,

kefula כְּפוּלָה, umaskurto וּמַשְׂכֻּרְתּוֹ pa'olo פָּעֳלוֹ vishalem וִישַׁלֵּם

(amen אָמֵן) lemala לְמַעְלָה lemala לְמַעְלָה veyitnehu וְיִתְּנֵהוּ

Tiferet   תפארת

hanimol הַנִּמּוֹל rach רַךְ yevarech יְבָרֵךְ hu הוּא harachaman, הָרַחֲמָן

laEl לָאֵל velibo וְלִבּוֹ yadav יָדָיו veyihyu וְיִהְיוּ lishmona לִשְׁמוֹנָה,

hashechinah הַשְּׁכִינָה, penei פְּנֵי lir'ot לִרְאוֹת veyizkeh וְיִזְכֶּה emunah אֱמוּנָה,

(amen אָמֵן) bashana בַּשָּׁנָה pe'amim פְּעָמִים shalosh שָׁלֹשׁ

The compassionate One! May He bless the father and mother of the child; may they merit to raise him, to train him, and to educate him to be a scholar. From the eighth day onward his blood is accepted; may the Lord, his God, be with him. The compassionate One! May He bless the sandek at the circumcision, who happily performed this good deed in joy. May He reward his deed and double his recompense and exalt him higher and higher. The compassionate One! May He bless the tender infant who has been circumcised on the eighth day; may his hands and heart be faithful to the Almighty, and may he merit to behold the Divine Presence three times a year.

Netzach / נצח

הָרַחֲמָן, harachaman, הוּא hu, יְבָרֵךְ yevarech, הַמָּל hamal, בְּשַׂר besar

הָעָרְלָה ha'orla, וּפָרַע ufara, וּמָצַץ umatzatz, דְּמֵי deme, הַמִּילָה hamila, אִישׁ ish

הַיָּרֵא hayare, וְרָךְ verach, הַלֵּבָב halevav, עֲבוֹדָתוֹ avodato, פְּסוּלָה pesula,

אִם im, שָׁלֹשׁ shelosh, אֵלֶּה ele, לֹא lo, יַעֲשֶׂה ya'ase, לָהּ la. (אמן amen)

Hod / הוד

הָרַחֲמָן, harachaman,

הוּא hu, יִשְׁלַח yishlach, לָנוּ lanu, בִּמְשִׁיחוֹ meshicho, הוֹלֵךְ holech, תָּמִים tamim,

בִּזְכוּת bizchut, וְזָתַן chatan, לַמּוּלוֹת lamulot, דָּמִים damim, לְבַשֵּׂר levaser

בְּשׂוֹרוֹת besorot, טוֹבוֹת tovot, וְנִחוּמִים venichumim, לְעַם le'am, אֶחָד echad

מִפֻּזָר mefuzar, וּמְפֹרָד umeforad, בֵּין ben, הָעַמִּים ha'amim. (אמן amen)

Yesod / יסוד

הָרַחֲמָן, harachaman, הוּא hu, יִשְׁלַח yishlach, לָנוּ lanu

כֹּהֵן Kohen, צֶדֶק tzedek, אֲשֶׁר asher, לֻקַּח lukach, לְעֵילוֹם le'elom,

עַד ad, הוּכַן huchan, כִּסְאוֹ kise'o, כַּשֶּׁמֶשׁ kashemesh, וְיַהֲלוֹם veyahalom,

וַיָּלֶט vayalet, פָּנָיו panav, בְּאַדַּרְתּוֹ be'adarto, וַיִּגְלֹם vayiglom, בְּרִיתִי beriti

הָיְתָה hayta, אִתּוֹ ito, הַחַיִּים hachayim, וְהַשָּׁלוֹם vehashalom: (אמן amen)

The compassionate One! May He bless the mohel who performed the circumcision, the periah and metzitzah. If a timid or faint-hearted man fails to perform these three parts of the mitzvah, his service is invalid. The compassionate One! May He send us His Mashiach who walks in perfection, in merit of the grooms bloodshed of circumcision, to bring good tidings and consolations to the one nation dispersed and scattered among the nations. The compassionate One! May He send us [Elijah] the righteous priest, who was taken into concealment, until his seat resplendent as the sun and precious stones is prepared for him; who covered his face with his mantle and enwrapped himself, with whom was made My covenant of life and peace.

for Shabbat:

הָרַחֲמָן, harachaman   הוּא hu   יַנְחִילֵנוּ yanchilenu   יוֹם yom   שֶׁכֻּלוֹ shekulo

שַׁבָּת Shabbat   וּמְנוּחָה umenuchah   לְחַיֵּי lechaye   הָעוֹלָמִים ha'olamim◆

for Rosh Chodesh:

הָרַחֲמָן, harachaman   הוּא hu   יְחַדֵּשׁ yechadesh   עָלֵינוּ alenu   אֵת et

הַחֹדֶשׁ hachodesh   הַזֶּה haze   לְטוֹבָה letova   וְלִבְרָכָה velivracha◆

for Holiday:

הָרַחֲמָן, harachaman

הוּא hu   יַנְחִילֵנוּ yanchilenu   יוֹם yom   שֶׁכֻּלוֹ shekulo   טוֹב tov◆

for Rosh Hashanah:

הָרַחֲמָן, harachaman   הוּא hu   יְחַדֵּשׁ yechadesh   עָלֵינוּ alenu

אֵת et   הַשָּׁנָה hashana   הַזֹּאת hazot   לְטוֹבָה letova   וְלִבְרָכָה velivracha◆

for Sukkot:

הָרַחֲמָן, harachaman   הוּא hu

יָקִים yakim   לָנוּ lanu   אֵת et   סֻכַּת sukkat   דָּוִד David   הַנּוֹפָלֶת hanofelet◆

On Shabbath:

The compassionate One!
May He cause us to inherit the day, which will be completely a Shabbath and rest day for eternal life.
On Rosh Chodesh: *The compassionate One! May He renew for us this month for good and for blessing.*
On Holidays: *The compassionate One! May He let us inherit that day which is all good.*
On Rosh Hashanah: *The compassionate One! May He renew for us this year for good and for blessing.*
On Sukkot: *The compassionate One! May He restore for us the fallen succah of David.*

הָרַחֲמָן, harachaman   הוא hu   יְזַכֵּנוּ yezakenu   לִימוֹת limot

הַמָּשִׁיחַ hamashi'ach   וּלְחַיֵּי ulchaye   הָעוֹלָם ha'olam   הַבָּא haba

מִגְדּוֹל migdol   יְשׁוּעוֹת yeshu'ot   מַלְכּוֹ malko   וְעוֹשֶׂה ve'ose   חֶסֶד chesed

לִמְשִׁיחוֹ limshicho   לְדָוִד leDavid   וּלְזַרְעוֹ ulezar'o   עַד ad   עוֹלָם olam

עוֹשֶׂה ose   שָׁלוֹם shalom   בִּמְרוֹמָיו bimromav   הוא hu   יַעֲשֶׂה ya'ase

שָׁלוֹם, shalom   עָלֵינוּ alenu   וְעַל ve'al   כָּל kol   יִשְׂרָאֵל, Yisrael

וְאִמְרוּ ve'imru   אָמֵן amen   יִרְאוּ yir'u   אֶת et   יְהוָה Adonai

קְדֹשָׁיו, kedoshav   כִּי ki   אֵין en   מַחְסוֹר machsor   לִירֵאָיו lire'av

כְּפִירִים kefirim   רָשׁוּ rashu   וְרָעֵבוּ vera'evu   וְדֹרְשֵׁי vedorshe

יְהוָה Adonai   לֹא lo   יַחְסְרוּ yach'seru   כָל kol   טוֹב tov   הוֹדוּ hodu

לַיהוָה ladonai   כִּי ki   טוֹב tov   כִּי ki   לְעוֹלָם le'olam   חַסְדּוֹ chasdo

The compassionate one! May he make us worthy of the days of Mashiach and the life of the world to come. He who is a tower the salvation of His king of salvation to His kingand and does kindness for His anointed, to David and to his descendants forever. He who makes peace in His heights may He make peace upon us and upon all Israel. Now respond: Amen! Fear The Lord, you — His holy ones — for there is no deprivation for His reverent ones. Young lions may want and hunger, but those who seek The Lord will not lack any good. Give thanks to God for he is good. His kindness endures forever.

POTEACH ET YADECHA (see meditations on pg. 109-110)

פּוֹתֵחַ pote'ach אֶת et יָדֶךָ yadecha

פָאי סָאל וֹזתך דִיקָרְנוּסָא
אמן יָאהדוֹנהִי יוֹזהתוּכה

וּמַשְׂבִּיעַ umasbi'a לְכָל־ lechol וֹזִי chai רָצוֹן ratzon ר״ת רוזל:

בָּרוּך baruch הַגֶּבֶר hagever אֲשֶׁר asher יִבְטַוֹו yivtach

בַּיהוָֹה badonai וְהָיָה vehaya יְהוָֹה Adonai

מִבְטַוֹוֹ mivtacho נַעַר na'ar הָיִיתִי hayiti גַּם gam זָקַנְתִּי zakanti וְלֹא velo

רָאִיתִי ra'iti צַדִּיק tzadik נֶעֱזָב ne'ezav וְזַרְעוֹ vezar'o מְבַקֶּשׁ mevakesh

לָחֶם lachem: יְהוָֹה Adonai עֹוֹ oz לְעַמּוֹ leamo יִתֵּן yiten

יְהוָֹה Adonai יְבָרֵך yevarech אֶת et עַמּוֹ amo בַּשָׁלוֹם bashalom:

You open Your hand and satisfy the desire of every living thing. Blessed is the man who trusts in the Lord, then the Lord will be his security. I was a youth and also have aged, and I have not seen a righteous man forsaken, with his children begging for bread. The Lord will give might to His people; The Lord will bless His people with peace.

LAST BLESSING – ME'EN SHALOSH

Food conceals and reveals different sparks of Light needed for our daily spiritual work. By reciting a blessing before and after we eat, we activate and elevate these sparks.

As we recite specific blessings for the different foods before we eat, so too there are different blessings that are recited after we have eaten. The following blessing is recited after eating food that was produced from the seven species of the land of Israel (food containing wheat, barley, rye, oats or spelt, grapes, wine or grape juice, figs, pomegranates, dates and olives). The "land of Israel" is a code name for the source and origin of the energy in our world. Reciting this blessing helps us to reconnect with the source.

baruch בָּרוּךְ   Ata אַתָּה   יְהֹוָאדֹנִיאַהדֹונֹהִי Adonai

Elohenu אֱלֹהֵינוּ   melech מֶלֶךְ   ha'olam הָעוֹלָם,   al עַל

On food from five grains:
(Wheat, barley, rye, oats & spelt)

hamichya הַמִּחְיָה   ve'al וְעַל   hakalkala הַכַּלְכָּלָה

On wine / grapejuice:

hagefen הַגֶּפֶן   ve'al וְעַל   hagefen הַגֶּפֶן   peri פְּרִי

On five fruits of the tree:
(Grapes, figs, pomegranates, dates, olives)

ha'etz הָעֵץ   ve'al וְעַל   ha'etz הָעֵץ   peri פְּרִי

On wine / grapejuice and food from five grains:

hamichya הַמִּחְיָה   ve'al וְעַל   hakalkala הַכַּלְכָּלָה

ve'al וְעַל   hagefen הַגֶּפֶן   ve'al וְעַל   peri פְּרִי   hagefen הַגֶּפֶן

Blessed are You, Lord our God, King of the universe
On food from five grains: *for the food and for the sustenance.*
On wine or grape juice: *for the vine and for the fruit of grapevine.*
On five Fruits: *for the trees and for the fruit of the trees.*
On Wine and Pastries: *for the food and for the sustenance and for the vine and for the fruit of grapevine.*

וְעַל ve'al   תְּנוּבַת tenuvat   הַשָּׂדֶה hasade   וְעַל ve'al   אֶרֶץ eretz

וְחֶמְדָּה chemda   טוֹבָה tova   וּרְחָבָה ur'chava

שֶׁרָצִיתָ sheratzita   וְהִנְחַלְתָּ vehinchalta   לַאֲבוֹתֵינוּ la'avotenu

לֶאֱכֹל le'echol   מִפִּרְיָהּ mipirya   וְלִשְׂבּוֹעַ velisbo'a   מִטּוּבָהּ mituva◆

רַחֵם rachem   יְהֹוָה Adonai   אֱלֹהֵינוּ Elohenu   עָלֵינוּ alenu

וְעַל ve'al   יִשְׂרָאֵל Yisrael   עַמָּךְ amach   וְעַל ve'al   יְרוּשָׁלַיִם Yerushalayim

עִירָךְ irach   וְעַל ve'al   הַר har   צִיּוֹן Tzion   מִשְׁכַּן mishkan   כְּבוֹדָךְ kevodach◆

וְעַל ve'al   מִזְבְּחֽוֹךְ mizbachach◆   וְעַל ve'al   הֵיכָלָךְ hechalach◆

וּבְנֵה uvne   יְרוּשָׁלַיִם Yerushalayim   עִיר ir   הַקֹּדֶשׁ hakodesh

בִּמְהֵרָה bimhera   בְיָמֵינוּ veyamenu◆   וְהַעֲלֵנוּ veha'alenu   לְתוֹכָהּ letocha◆

וְשַׂמְּחֵנוּ vesamchenu   בְּבִנְיָנָהּ bevinyana◆   וּנְבָרֶכְךָ un'var'chach

עָלֶיהָ aleha   בִּקְדוּשָׁה bikdusha   וּבְטָהֳרָה uv'tahara◆

And for the produce of the field and for the fine, fertile and grate Land, that You have given our fathers as inheritance to eat of its crop and to be sated with its goodness. Be merciful The Lord, our God on Israel, your people, and on Jerusalem your city and on the mount Zion, the place of Your glory, and on the Altar and on your Temple. And reconstruct Jerusalem the Holy City speedily in our days and bring us there and gladden us with its rebuilding and we will bless You for it in holiness and purity.

For Shabbat:

וּרְצֵה urtze וְהַחֲלִיצֵנוּ vehachalitzenu בְּיוֹם beyom הַשַּׁבָּת haShabbat הַזֶּה haze.

For Rosh Chodesh:

וְזָכְרֵנוּ vezochrenu לְטוֹבָה letova בְּיוֹם beyom רֹאשׁ rosh הַחֹדֶשׁ hachodesh הַזֶּה haze.

For Rosh Hashanah:

וְזָכְרֵנוּ vezochrenu לְטוֹבָה letova בְּיוֹם beyom הַזִּכָּרוֹן hazikaron הַזֶּה haze.

For Pesach:

וְשַׂמְּחֵנוּ vesamchenu בְּיוֹם beyom וַזַּג chag הַמַּצּוֹת hamatzot הַזֶּה haze.

בְּיוֹם beyom (say on holiday: טוֹב tov) מִקְרָא mikra קֹדֶשׁ kodesh הַזֶּה haze.

For Shavuot:

וְשַׂמְּחֵנוּ vesamchenu בְּיוֹם beyom וַזַּג chag הַשָּׁבוּעוֹת haShavout הַזֶּה haze.

בְּיוֹם beyom טוֹב tov מִקְרָא mikra קֹדֶשׁ kodesh הַזֶּה haze.

For Sukkot:

וְשַׂמְּחֵנוּ vesamchenu בְּיוֹם beyom וַזַּג chag הַסֻּכּוֹת haSukkot הַזֶּה haze.

בְּיוֹם beyom (on holiday add: טוֹב tov) מִקְרָא mikra קֹדֶשׁ kodesh הַזֶּה haze.

For Simchat Torah:

וְשַׂמְּחֵנוּ vesamchenu בְּיוֹם beyom וַזַּג chag שְׁמִינִי Shemini עֲצֶרֶת Atzert.

הַזֶּה haze בְּיוֹם beyom טוֹב tov מִקְרָא mikra קֹדֶשׁ kodesh הַזֶּה haze.

On Shabbat: *and accept favorably and console us on this day of Shabbat*
On Rosh Chodesh: *and remember us on this day of the new moon*
On Rosh Hashana: *and remember us on this day of Remembrance*
On Pesach: *and bring us joy on this Matzot festival, on this day of holy convocation.*
On Shavuot: *and bring us joy on this festival of Shavuot, on this day of holy convocation.*
On Sukkot: *and bring us joy on this festival of Sukkot, on this day of holy convocation.*
On Shmini Atzeret: *and bring us joy on this festival of Shmini Atzeret, on this day of holy convocation.*

כִּי ki אַתָּה ata טוֹב tov וּמֵטִיב umetiv לַכֹּל lakol ‧ וְנוֹדֶה venode לְךָ lecha

יְהֹוָה(אדנייאהדונהי) Adonai אֱלֹהֵינוּ Elohenu עַל al הָאָרֶץ ha'aretz וְעַל ve'al

On food from five grains: הַמִּחְיָה hamichya וְעַל ve'al הַכַּלְכָּלָה hakalkala

On wine / grapejuice: פְּרִי peri הַגֶּפֶן hagefen

On five fruits of the tree: פְּרִי peri הָעֵץ ha'etz

בָּרוּךְ baruch אַתָּה Ata יְהֹוָה(אדנייאהדונהי) Adonai עַל al הָאָרֶץ ha'aretz וְעַל ve'al

On food from five grains: הַמִּחְיָה hamichya וְעַל ve'al הַכַּלְכָּלָה hakalkala

If the food is from Israel say this instead: מִחְיָתָהּ michyata וְעַל ve'al כַּלְכָּלָתָהּ kalkalata

On wine / grapejuice: פְּרִי peri הַגֶּפֶן hagefen

If the wine is from Israel say this instead: פְּרִי peri גַּפְנָהּ gafna

On five fruits of the tree: הַפֵּרוֹת haperot

If the fruit is from Israel say this instead: פֵּרוֹתֶיהָ peroteha

For You The Lord are good and do good to all, and we will bless You for the land and
On food from five grains: for the food.
On wine or grape juice: for the fruit of grapevine.
On five Fruits: for the fruit of the trees.
Blessed are You, Lord, for the land and
On food from five grains: for the food and for the sustenance.
On wine or grape juice: for the vine and for the fruit of grapevine.
On five Fruits: for the trees and for the fruit of the trees.

Last Blessing – Bore Nefashot

This blessing is recited over any other food.

melech מֶלֶךְ Elohenu אֱלֹהֵינוּ Adonai יְהֹוָה אלהייאהדונהי Ata אַתָּה baruch בָּרוּךְ

vechesronan וְחֶסְרוֹנָן, rabot רַבּוֹת nefashot נְפָשׁוֹת bore בּוֹרֵא ha'olam הָעוֹלָם

bahem בָּהֶם lehachayot לְהַחֲיוֹת shebarata שֶׁבָּרֵאתָ ma מַה kol כָּל al עַל

ha'olamim הָעוֹלָמִים chai וָזִי baruch בָּרוּךְ, chai וָזִי kol כָּל nefesh נֶפֶשׁ

Blessed are You,
Lord our God, King of the universe Who created many living things and all everything to satisfy their needs;
for all that You have created to maintain all life. Blessed is the One Who is the life of the worlds.

TRAVELING – *ALEF LAMED DALET*

INSIGHT

This name is for protection. Going on a trip creates an opening for negative energy to enter us.

MEDITATION

Scan the following section from the Zohar, Lech-Lecha before leaving the house to go on a trip on a plane, in the car, etc. Imagine that you are creating a shield of positive energy surrounding you, offering protection from any negativity.

◆ba'aretz בָּאָרֶץ Avram אַבְרָם vaya'avor וַיַּעֲבֹר ketiv כְּתִיב ma מַה chamei וְזִמֵי

hacha הָכָא, ela אֶלָּא, lei לֵיהּ miba'ei מִבָּעֵי veyelech וַיֵּלֶךְ, vaya'avor וַיַּעֲבֹר,

de'itchathim דְּאִתְוַזְהֵים, kadisha קַדִּישָׁא shema שְׁמָא remez רְמֵז hu הוּא

decholho דְּכָלְהוֹ gelifan גְּלִיפָן atvan אַתְוָון be'ayin bet בְּע"ב alma עָלְמָא bei בֵּיהּ

uchtiv וּכְתִיב, vaya'avor וַיַּעֲבֹר hacha הָכָא ketiv כְּתִיב ◆da דָּא bishma בִּשְׁמָא

◆vayikra וַיִּקְרָא panav פָּנָיו al עַל hashem ה' vaya'avor וַיַּעֲבֹר hatam הָתָם

66. *See, it is written, "And Abram passed through the land."* HE ASKS, WHY DOES THE VERSE READ, *"Passed through (Heb. vaya'avor)" instead of 'went'! This is an allusion to the Holy Name – by which the world is sealed – that contains 72 engraved letters, all of which are within that name.* VAYA'AVOR (VAV-YUD-AYIN-BET- RESH) CONSISTS OF TWO PARTS – RESH-YUD-VAV (=216) AND AYIN-BET (=72) – THAT REFER TO THE 216 LETTERS AND 72 NAMES. *Thus, it is written in one place, "And...passed through," while it is written in another, "And Hashem passed by (Heb. vaya'avor) before him and proclaimed..."* – JUST AS THERE IT IS SPEAKING OF THE HOLY NAME OF AYIN-BET, SO TOO VAYA'AVOR HERE IS A REFERENCE TO THE HOLY NAME OF AYIN-BET (72).

◀   Scanning Direction

THE 72 NAMES OF GOD

The 72 Names of God are not "names" in the ordinary sense. They are very different from the signature on a letter or the back of a credit card. Instead, they are channels of the Infinite spiritual current that flows through the world.

By connecting to these sources of spiritual power, we acquire protection from any and all forms of negativity and danger. We remove the blockages that separate us from total joy and fulfillment. We open the pathways to transformation – for ourselves and for the entire world.

8	7	6	5	4	3	2	1	
כהת	אכא	ללה	מהש	עלם	סיט	ילי	והו	A
הקם	הרי	מבה	יזל	ההע	לאו	אלד	הזי	B
וזהו	מלה	ייי	נלך	פהל	לוו	כלי	לאו	C
ועור	לכב	אום	ריי	שאה	ירת	האא	נתה	D
ייז	רהע	וזעם	אני	מנד	כוק	להו	יוז	E
מיה	עשל	ערי	סאל	ילה	וול	מיכ	ההה	F
פוי	מבה	נית	ננא	עממ	הוש	דני	והו	G
בוזי	ענו	יהה	ומב	מצר	הרח	ייל	נמם	H
מום	היי	יבמ	ראה	וזבו	איע	מנק	דמב	I

For more information call 1-800-kabbalah (1-800-522-2252)

The explanations and prayers in this book are tools to help you on your journey toward becoming master of your own destiny. Through the use and understanding of these tools, you will discover your God-given birthright — happiness, joy, fulfillment, and peace on earth.

Kabbalah teaches us never to simply accept what we are told by others. Instead, we are asked to be open-minded and to try Kabbalah's technology to see if it works for us. As with any technology, the more we understand, the more we can accomplish. Apply the tools that are provided in this book and watch your life improve.

For more information, books, courses, and student support, call:
1-800-kabbalah (1-800-522-2252)

Or go to our website at
www.kabbalah.com

Or call The Kabbalah Centre near you.

Centres in USA
Boca Raton, FL 561 488 8826
Los Angeles, CA 310 657 5404
Miami, FL 305 692 9223
New York, NY 212 644 0025

International Centres
London, England 44 207 499 4974
Mexico City, Mexico 525 555 89 44 64
Toronto, Canada 416 631 9395
Tel Aviv, Israel 972 3 52 66 800

PEOPLE

Rav and Karen

Current directors of The Kabbalah Centre, Rav and Karen Berg are the first
people in history to make the teachings of Kabbalah available to anyone with a sincere desire to learn.

Rabbi Eliezer

The son of Rabbi Shimon bar Yochai, the author of the Zohar.

Rabbi Bachye Iben Paquda

Kabbalist who wrote the book *Chovat Halevavot* (*Duties of the Heart*).

Rav Isaac Luria (the Ari)

16th century kabbalist (1534 - 1572), he was called *HaAri* (the Lion) by his students. He revolutionized the study of Kabbalah through his understanding and explanation of the concepts.

Rabbi Nachunya ben Hakana

2nd century kabbalist who was the first to reveal the 42-letter Name of God,
providing us with the *Ana Beko'ach*, the world's most powerful prayer.

WORDS AND PHRASES

Aramaic letters

The Aramaic letters in this book are more than just the basis of words and language. Their actual shape and form is designed to channel the creative force of Light into our world and our lives. Scanning (from right to left) is all we need to experience the effect of prayer.

Kavanah, Kavanot

The intent and meditation that accompany the words of prayer. Intent gives the mind direction and purpose. According to the Zohar, *kavanah* is a significant and integral element of spiritual growth.

Kohen

Priest. The channel healing energy in our world.

Lightforce, Light

The Lightforce or the Light is the kabbalistic term for the emanation of the essence and character of the Creator. This essence is one of sharing, in which aspects of negativity simply do not exist. Just as the light from a single candle will dispel the darkness, the Lightforce of the Creator will dispel chaos, pain, and suffering from our lives and our world.

Living water

Water is the physical expression of the Light of the Creator. Living water springs upward from underground wells. It is said that all wells on earth are connected.

Negative shells

Each time we behave in a reactive manner or make negative choices, we build a layer of darkness around ourselves. Kabbalists refer to these layers as *klippot*, or "shells." It is these shells that separate us from the Lightforce.

Numerical value

Each Aramaic letter is also a number. By determining the numerical value of a word, we can learn more about that word by studying other words with the same numerical value.

Prayer

Kabbalistically, prayer is a means by which humanity can participate in the dynamics of the cosmos. Prayer is a precise technology made up of both action and speech.

Root word

Root words, composed of three or possibly four letters, provide the basis for understanding all words with the same root.

Sefer Yitzerah

Written by Abraham the Patriarch, *Sefer Yitzerah* ("*The Book of Formation*") is the oldest of all kabbalistic texts. The entire book is only a few pages long and is a code containing the secrets of astrology and the significance of the Aramaic letters.

Sefira, Sefirot

There are ten *Sefirot*, or ten dimensions, in our universe. The word *Sefirot* literally means "emanations." As the Lightforce of the Creator moves from its source (the Godhead) into our world, it passes through a series of 'curtains,' or *Sefirot* (singular, *Sefirah*), each of which filters the amount of Light passing through to the next level until all Light has been filtered out and we arrive at our world filled with darkness. The essence of the Light has not changed: Only the amount that is revealed is different. By learning about the *Sefirot* and their purpose, we can increase the amount of Light revealed in our lives.

Spiritual purification

What separates us from or connects us to the Creator is our affinity with the Creator. Through millennia of reactive behavior and negative choices, mankind has created layers of separation between itself and the Creator. By removing these layers, we experience spiritual purification, developing more and more affinity with the Lightforce and the Creator.

Tetragrammaton יְהֹוָה

The Tetragrammaton (Greek for "the four letters") is the most powerful Name of God. The Name itself is not pronounced. It is sometimes referred to as *Yud Hei Vav Hei* or *Yud Kei Vav Kei*.

The Satan

The powerful, intelligent force that opposes our actions to reveal Light. It is the existence of this force that guarantees that mankind will develop the power of free will and choice.

Tree of Knowledge of Good and Evil reality

Kabbalah and science teach that there are parallel universes. The Tree of Knowledge of Good and Evil reality is the world in which we live — a world filled with chaos, pain, and suffering.

Tree of Life reality

Kabbalah and science teach that there are parallel universes. The Tree of Life reality is the Flawless Universe, where pain, suffering, and chaos do not exist.

Zohar

Written in Aramaic, the Zohar contains the teachings of Rav Shimon bar Yochai and explanations of the hidden meaning of the Five Books of Moses, the Torah. The Zohar is our doorway to a life filled with the Lightforce of the Creator.